Best wishes to my friend
Bill McCole.

Frank Leu

WAR DIARY
OF THE
27TH FIGHTER SQUADRON

As Recorded by Intelligence Personnel

Comments by
Frank Lawson, Col. USAF (Ret.)

GATEWAY PRESS, INC.
Baltimore, MD   1997

Copyright © 1997 by Frank Lawson, Col. USAF (Ret.)

All rights reserved.
Permission to reproduce in any form
must be secured from the author.

Please direct all correspondence and book orders to:
Frank Lawson
3164 Gatsby Lane
Montgomery, AL 36106

Library of Congress Catalog Card Number 97-74236
ISBN 0-9660974-0-8

Published for the author by
Gateway Press, Inc.
1001 N. Calvert Street
Baltimore, MD 21202

Printed in the United States of America

Dedication

TO THOSE MEMBERS OF
THE 27TH SQUADRON
WHO NEVER HAD
THE REWARDS OF OLD AGE
AND
TO MY LOVING WIFE
"SARAH"

THE 27ᵀᴴ FIGHTER SQUADRON

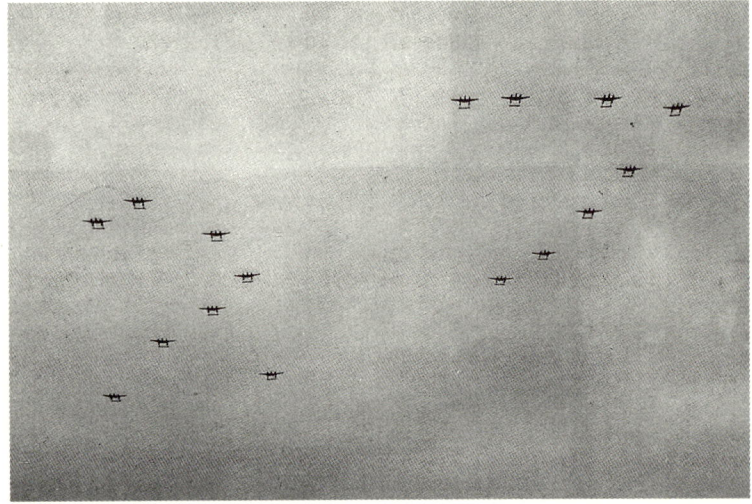

Everyone likes to show off occasionally and fighter pilots are no exception. The number "27" took a little imagination. (Bob Share)

WAR DIARY OF THE 27TH FIGHTER SQUADRON

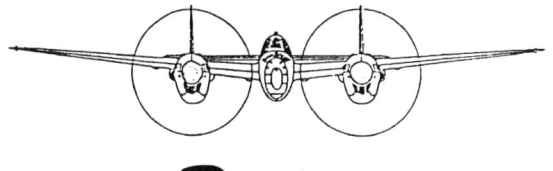

Preface

From its origin in May 1917 until this date, the 27th has served with distinction. As the oldest fighter squadron in the Air Force, it is currently based at Langley Air Force Base in Virginia and operates the F-15 "Eagle" in any part of the world to which it is ordered.

A diary often consists of one's personal thoughts and recollections consigned to the pages of a locked book, where they remain until after the death of the writer. This, however, is the record of daily happenings in an Army Air Corps fighter squadron during the period from August 1943 until May 1944. There is no format or rule which determined what was entered and what was left out, only the judgement and available time of the individual making the entry for that particular day. The diary was the responsibility of the intelligence section which consisted of two officers and several "intell" technicians, any one of whom may have made each days entry. Several "country store" type ledgers contain these hand written diaries which are on file at the Air Force Historical Research Agency, located at Maxwell Air Force Base, Alabama.

COMMENTS: are offered after each day's entry where my military flight records and personal memory are able to provide details. The events described here were the most dramatic which had occurred in my life and, as a nineteen-year-old second lieutenant, they made a lasting impression. The personality and unique nature of any military organization is in its people. Historical "facts" can become dry statistics to some, but they are all very much a part of the heart and soul of those who shared in these events.

27th FIGHTER SQUADRON
GROUP PICTURE, JAN. 20, 1944
SALSOLA AIRFIELD — FOGGIA, ITALY

Front Row

1st. Lt. Walter F. Flynn
1st. Lt. James S. Alford
1st. Lt. Marvin V. Wingrove
1st. Lt. Arden W. Ferrin
1st. Lt. Francis J. Maron
Capt. Gilbert E. Butler (C.O.)
1st. Lt. Thomas F. Rafael (Ops)
1st. Lt. Larry O. Reynolds
1st. Lt. Warren P. Eickmann
1st. Lt. James B. Meikle

Middle Row

1st. Lt. Francis R. Lawson
2nd. Lt. Merle B. Brown**
1st. Lt. Lester C. Peterson
1st. Lt. Lester H. Laird
2nd. Lt. Robert E. Austin
2nd. Lt. Frank J. Gerry**
2nd. Lt. Armour C. Miller
2nd. Lt. Robert L. McIntosh*
1st. Lt. Frederick D. Nichol
2nd. Lt. Thomas P. Prout

Back Row

2nd. Lt. Robert C. Burgoyne
2nd. Lt. Richard A. Cooley*
2nd. Lt. Harold F. Lindiurst**
2nd. Lt. John H. Price***
2nd. Lt. David J. Fischer*
2nd. Lt. Thomas E. Maloney***
2nd. Lt. Harold N. Lienau
F/O Edward R. Morgan
F/O Ronald C. Delaney**
2nd. Lt. Kenneth E. Hartwig*
2nd. Lt. William G. Parsons*
2nd. Lt. James L. Rodolff*

* Did not survive the war
** POW - survived the war
*** Wounded in action

Prepared by Thomas E. Maloney

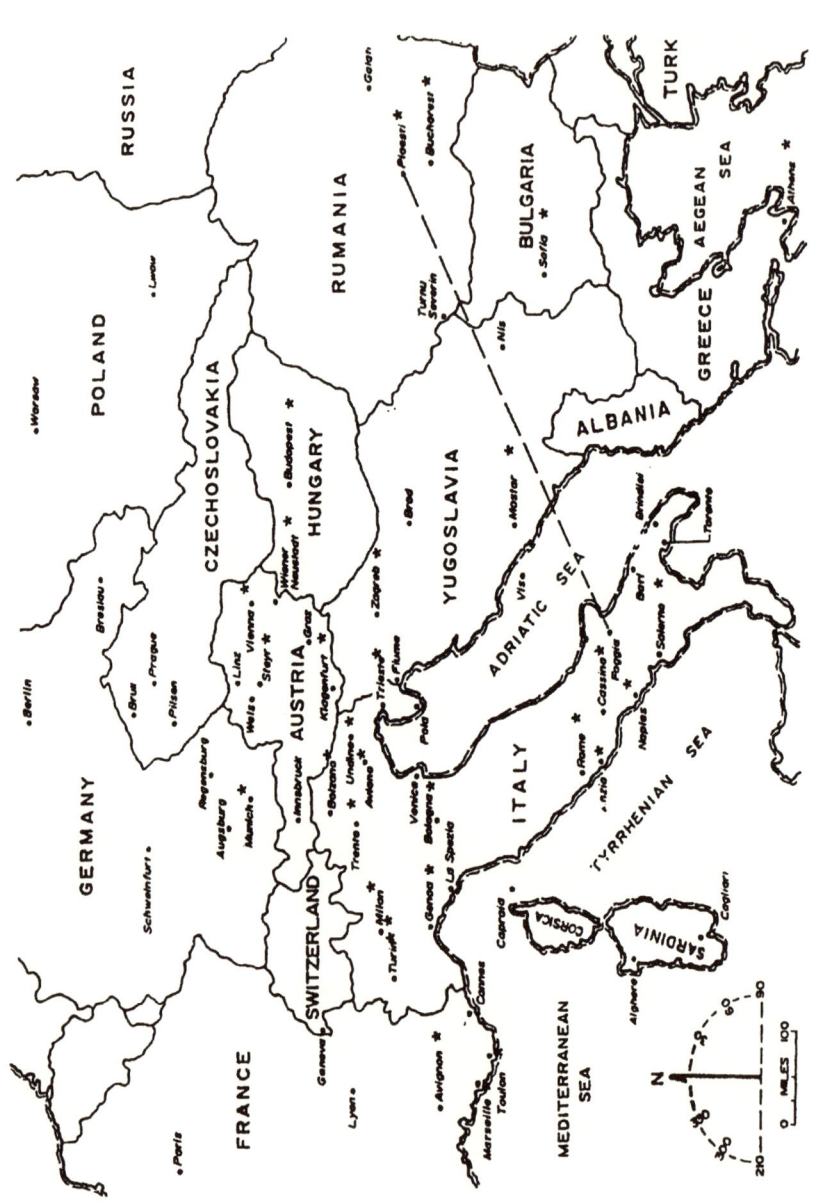

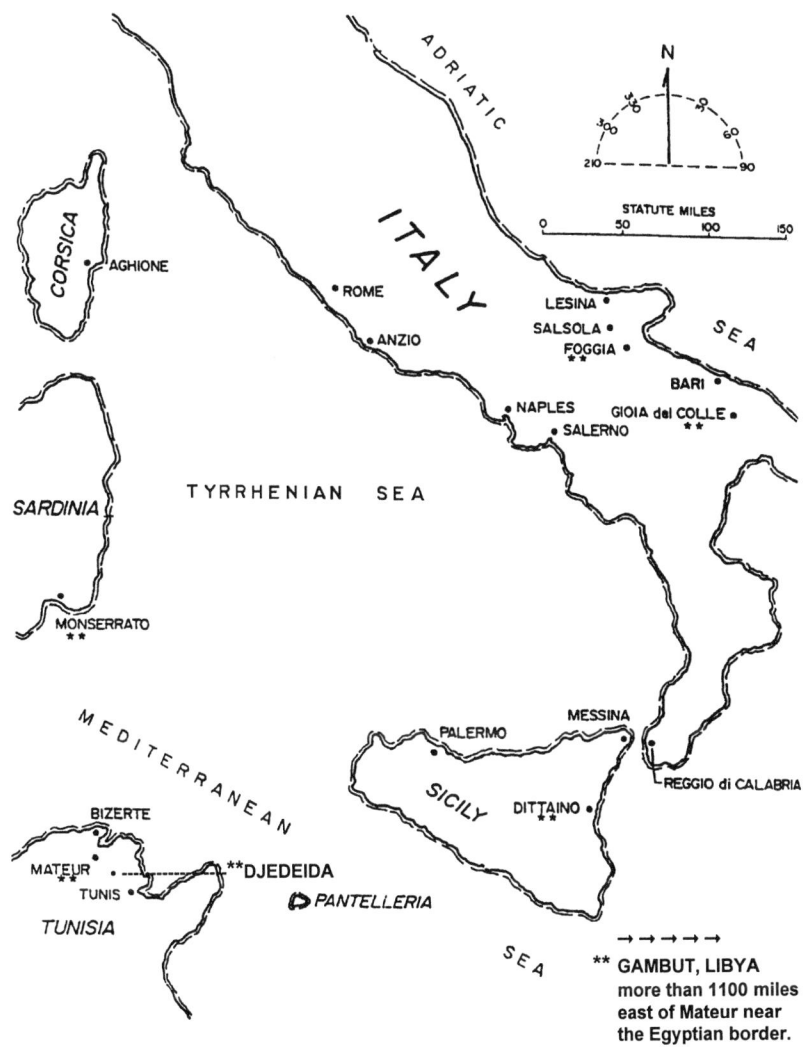

** BASED IN THESE AREAS

ACKNOWLEDGEMENTS

Thanks to:

Brigadier General T.W. Lay, II, Commander of the 1st Fighter Wing, who first encouraged me to take on the publication of this War Diary.

Ms. Jane N. Grider who labored through my first draft and produced this finished copy.

My friends who patiently listened, read, and encouraged me to "press on."

WAR DIARY OF THE 27TH FIGHTER SQUADRON

*August 20, 1943
through
April 23, 1944*

WAR DEPARTMENT
A. A. F. Form No. 5
(Revised)

INDIVIDUAL FLIGHT RECORD

NAME **FRANCIS R. LAWSON**　　　　　　　　　　MONTH(S) **August**, 19**43**
RANK **2nd Lt., A.C.**　　　　　　　　　　　　　GROUP **1st Fighter Group**
AERO. RATINGS **Pilot**　　　　　　　　　　　　ORGANIZATION—Assigned **27th Fighter Squadron**
TRANSFERRED FROM **439th F.Sq., 3rd F. Command**　ORG.—Attached for flying
TO **1st F. G., 27th F. Sq.** DATE　　　　　　　STATION **APO # 520**

1	2	3	4						5	6	7	8
Date	Duty	Mission Symbol	PILOT TIME BY AIRPLANE TYPE						Aircraft Model Symbol	No. of Landings	Other Than Pilot	REMARKS
			Attack	Bomb.	Obs.	Pursuit	Cargo	Training				
26	P	A				0:45			F-38G	1		Mateur-Local
27	P	A				1:15			"	1		" "
27	P	A				1:00			F-38F	1		Mateur-Local
28	P	A				0:45			"	1		" "
28	P	A				0:30			F-38G	1		" "
29	P	A				1:00			"	1		" "
30	P	A				2:45			"	2		" "
31	P	A				2:30			"	4		Mat-Bizerte-Mateur

									9	10	11	12
TOTALS									Total pilot time	Total other than pilot	Pilot time nonmilitary airplane	
This report						10:30			10:30		10:30	
Previous reports this F.Y.						47:20			47:20		45:15	
Totals this fiscal year						57:50			57:50		55:45	
Totals previous years						219:25			219:25			
Totals to date						277:15			277:15			

*DUTY SYMBOLS
P—Pilot　　B—Bomber　　R—Radio operator
CP—Copilot　　OB—Observer　　PH—Photographer
N—Navigator　　E—Engineer　　O—Other crew
C—Command Pilot　G—Gunner　　X—Passenger

DUPLICATE

NOTE.—When the airplane is assigned to an organization other than that to which the individual is assigned or attached for flying, show the airplane organization under Remarks, column 8.

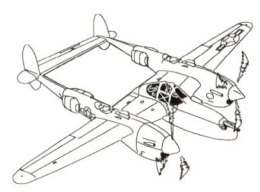# WAR DIARY OF THE 27ᵀᴴ FIGHTER SQUADRON

August 1943

20 TH — Fourteen of our P-38s went with the 71st and 94th Squadrons to escort B-26s which were to bomb Caserta Railroad Junction, Italy. Ten minutes before going into the target, the formation was attacked by fifty or more enemy fighters. All through the target, and for fifteen minutes afterwards, a general dogfight ensued. Our fellows claimed four destroyed and four probably destroyed. F/O Styer, Lt. Eickmann, F/O Deisenroth, and Lt. Randel got a "destroyed" each. We also lost two of our pilots, Lts. Webb and Post. Neither was seen to come out of the target area. Both were very good pilots who had shown a lot of promise in the few times they had flown with the squadron. Lt. Post, who closely resembled Capt. Runyon, was very young, only nineteen years old, the youngest pilot we have had. A quiet, likable kid, he was very popular with everyone who got to know him in the short time he was with us. We had another heat spell and today around the middle of the day all records must have been broken.

21 ST — Yesterday's score was changed to give us one more "destroyed" and one more "damaged," with two less "probables." Lts. Tibble and Ferrin shared credit for the one destroyed. Today was a repetition of yesterday, almost. Twenty of our P-38s, escorting B-26s to Villa Literno Railroad Yards in Italy, were jumped by fifteen to twenty enemy aircraft. This time our pilots came out on top, destroying three of the enemy without loss to themselves. One other was claimed as probably destroyed and four were damaged. All of our planes returned safely. Nothing else of special interest happened in the squadron today. The heat continues, and today was a real scorcher.

22ND There was no mission scheduled for today. A number of the pilots went up on local training flights. Capt. Duke received a letter from Lt. Shaw's sister saying that the lieutenent was a prisoner of war. Lt. Shaw has been missing since he went on a mission to Sardinia on the 5th of June. It was unusually warm all day and stayed that way through most of the night. Lts. Smith and Smythe returned from rest camp today. Major Kirtley and Lt. McQuown took off on a cross-country flight to Gibraltar this morning.

23RD The only mission today was an early morning Air Sea Rescue job. Six of our planes went out on it, but only three completed the mission. They escorted a Catalina which made no sightings. Just before daybreak we had a paratroop alert and a double guard was put on, but nothing happened. Our planes did some practice night flying this evening. That is to be the regular thing for awhile, it is rumored. Lt. McIntosh returned from rest camp this afternoon. Six new pilots joined the squadron today and were assigned as of today, also. They are 1st Lt. James S. Alford, 2nd Lts. Eldon E. Vondra, Merle B. Brown, Frank J. Gerry, Jr., Francis R. Lawson, and Walter J. Flynn.

COMMENTS 8/23/43: First impressions are usually lasting and as one of the six new pilots assigned this date, that memory is still quite clear. The squadron was based on a dry lake bed (dry until the rains began) just outside the little town of Mateur, about 40 miles inland from the port city of Bizerte, Tunisia. Everyone was reasonably friendly, but there was a "no nonsense" attitude which made it clear that the drills, training, and such were a thing of the past. Before we even had a place to unroll our gear, Lt. Butler, the operations officer, sat us down in the intelligence tent and had us read a copy of the squadron history. The 27th was and still is the oldest fighter squadron in the Air Force, dating back to May 1917. Pride in the squadron ran deep and we were expected to "measure up."

The nearest shower facility was more than ten miles away and it soon became obvious that maintaining a level of cleanliness in the heat and dust of North Africa, so that we could stand each other, would be a major problem.

24 TH

No mission today. A few of the pilots went up on local training flights. The enlisted men are restricted to the camp area until further notice. We had a special treat of coffee and cake just before dark. This was a beautiful day, not too warm, and there wasn't a cloud in the sky. Major Kirtley and Lt. McQuown returned from their trip to Gibraltar.

COMMENTS 8/24/43: The six of us who were assigned yesterday had never flown a P-38, and I had never even seen one. So, how we came to be assigned to the 27th is a story worth telling now. After some sixty or seventy hours of training in Florida on P-40s we were sent to North Africa to join a P-40 squadron already there. Upon reaching Tunis, we found that our squadron had been deactivated and was moving to the 9th Air Force, which left us with no assignment. The "old man" of our group, 1st Lt. Jim Alford, had been an instructor at an advanced flying school and, by chance, met his former commander, now a senior officer at 12th Air Force Headquarters. Jim explained our situation whereupon he was asked if any of us had "any multi-engine experience." Ever wary of being diverted to the "right seat" of some transport aircraft, Jim replied no, we were all fighter pilots. His friend went on to explain that the P-38 units (multi-engine fighters) were badly in need of replacement pilots. Everyone wanted to fly P-38s and Lt. Alford promptly reasoned that since we had all flown from the States to North Africa in the back of a four-engine transport; we all indeed had "multi-engine" experience. A random chance meeting had now permanently altered the course of our lives and, with this stroke of good fortune, we were now in the 27th Fighter Squadron.

25 TH

One of the biggest days the squadron has had since being in operation. We had felt for the last two days that something big was coming up, and so it did. Twenty-four of our planes went with a like number from both the 71st and 94th Squadrons, and a like number from each squadron of the 82nd and 14th Groups. Two hundred sixteen P-38s, in all, went to ground strafe the enemy's big airfield at Foggia in central Italy. The raid was so carefully planned and so neatly executed that the Jerries were taken completely by surprise and great damage was done. Our fellows alone accounted for twenty-three JU-88s and one JU-52 destroyed. One JU-88 and one single engine fighter were probably destroyed. Twenty-three JU-88s and two S/E fighters were damaged. A great number of casualties to personnel working on the planes were observed. Besides this attack, they also strafed a large troop train, inflicting heavy casualties among those who were waiting to board the train in a station. We suffered the loss of one pilot and one plane. Lt. Williams' right engine caught fire going over the target and he was forced to bail out right there over the target. His chute opened and he was seen to hit the ground. Lt. Brown paid us a visit this afternoon. He has been in the hospital here in Tunisia since he was brought back from Sicily after his very narrow escape on June 11th. He had quite an experience, and he was called on to tell his story a number of times. It goes something like this:

"After I bailed out and hit the ground I threw my parachute and Mae West into the flames of my burning plane which had crashed nearby. I heard bullets whizzing by my head and realized I was being pursued so I sought the shelter of a nearby woods where I spent the night. In the morning I went out on the road, intending to head south and try and reach Syracuse, somehow. I passed an Italian sentry unmolested by giving him the Nazi salute and a 'Heil Hitler.' Shortly after that, however, I was captured by a group of Italian soldiers, who walked me almost ten miles to an Italian army post, where, after being questioned a great many times, I got partial treatment for my badly burnt face and arm. I remained there all night, and in the morning I was taken to Catania by truck. Upon arrival there I was turned over to the Italian Air Force Headquarters. There, I was given food and water. We had an air raid shortly after that, and I was then told that the headquarters was preparing to move to Messina and evacuate to Italy. On the way to Messina I realized that if they got me over to Italy my chances of escape would be very slim, so I complained of my arm and asked them to take me to a hospital. I was taken to the Messina Naval Hospital where I met with an Italian baroness, who was an International Red Cross worker. She treated me very kindly and I had good care though the food was poor. I stayed in that hospital for two weeks, during which time we were frequently bombed, as the hospital was situated right near the beach where a lot of the German and Italian barges going across the Straits landed and embarked. When the Allies started bombarding the city with artillery fire, we were evacuated to a haven up in the hills overlooking the Straits. There I met three British officers who had been captured at Catania. Together with them I persuaded the commandant of the hospital to surrender the place to us, telling him that he wouldn't be in such a difficult position when the Allies finally captured the place. He consented to this and ordered the personnel to turn over their weapons to us. We, however, already had all their guns which we had taken while they sought shelter in an air raid. Finally, on August 17, an American medical officer and his staff arrived and took over. The next day we were on our way back to Africa on a C-47 and on arriving there I was put in a hospital just outside Mateur. It was from there that I finally contacted my friends at the 27th."

COMMENTS 8/25/43: Although a nonparticipant in today's operation, I was immensely proud of just being a part of this squadron. At the time, I failed to grasp the enormity of what had been accomplished but, even so, I was envious of those who were involved. Several individual decorations and awards resulted from this mission, not the least of which was a Presidential Unit Citation for the entire 1st Fighter Group.

26 TH

Twenty-one of our P-38s went with the B-26s who bombed Grazzanise A/D, Italy. The results were not observed because dust obscured the target area. A few enemy aircraft made a couple of halfhearted attacks on the formation, but there were no claims made and all of our planes returned safely. The paratroops who were thought to be dropped the other night turned up in a couple of places around us and two of them were captured just across the road from us. They said their objective was to destroy the P-38s on this field. A twenty-four hour guard on all the planes will be maintained from now on.

COMMENTS 8/26/43: If there was any doubt that this was the "real thing," the paratroop incident put all that to rest. On a personal level, the big thing today was my first flight in a P-38. The truly amazing fact is that the squadron put up twenty-one aircraft on a combat mission and still managed to provide training flights for us new pilots.

Lt. Purvis, whose name frequently appears in this diary, was my instructor. He had completed his combat missions but remained in the squadron to do a number of very worthwhile assignments. We had no "piggyback" airplane at this time, so Lt. Purvis sat on the wing and carefully put me through a lengthy drill about what to do and how to do it. After what seemed like hours I was finally ready to "fire it up" and go. Fearful is not the word, but I was apprehensive because I wanted so desperately to do well and not "mess up." Looking back over fifty years and thousands of hours of flying, this was without a doubt the "high point." Just a few of the adjectives which come to mind are: "honest," "forgiving," "powerful," "responsive," and "all in all, wonderful" airplane. Just how wonderful, I would find out later. Unlike other aircraft, the propellers on the P-38 both rotated in opposite directions, thus eliminating any torque. This fact, plus better forward visibility and a tricycle landing gear, actually made it easier to fly than a P-40. I loved it!

27 TH

Nineteen of our planes escorted B-26s to Caserta Railroad Yards, Italy. Over the target, twenty to twenty-five enemy aircraft appeared and, though none of them were very aggressive, they did press home one attack which damaged one of our planes and injured Lt. Laird. Lt. Laird nevertheless destroyed the enemy plane, which was an ME-109. Lt. Randol damaged another. Lt. Laird, having one engine shot out, made a crash landing on the beach at Bizerte. He was taken to a hospital there. All of our other planes returned safely to the base. Today was especially hot. The skies were clear and not a cloud could be seen. The enlisted men of the squadron carried on their usual duties. The new pilots went up on local training flights.

28 TH

Our P-38s escorted B-26s to Aversa Railway Yards, Italy. They encountered about thirty enemy planes in the target area. One flight of ours covered the bombers while they made their run, while the others engaged the enemy. Lt. Smythe destroyed an MA-202, and Lt. Hurst destroyed an FW-190. We had no losses, and all of our planes landed safely at the base. The results of the bombing were not observed. We heard some more details about Lt. Laird's "darn good job" of bringing his ship in as far as he did. He flew over 350 miles of water on one engine after he had been wounded by a 20mm shell that exploded in his cockpit. All of the men of the squadron went through the gas chamber this morning.

29 TH

Sixteen of our planes escorted B-26s to Torre Annuziata, Italy. The pilots, upon their return, said they ran into the "first team of the Luftwaffe," today. Thirty-five to forty enemy aircraft were engaged over the target area and fifty miles out to sea, after fighting through the bomb run and all. The enemy flew excellent formation, and were very aggressive. One of our P-38s was destroyed. The pilot, Lt. Graham, bailed out over the water, and he was seen later down in the water. An Air Sea Rescue was dispatched from Sicily to pick him up. As yet we haven't heard anything more about him. Lt. Smythe and F/O Wennergren each claimed a damaged. Today was very cool and we had a strong wind which threatened to blow down the tents in camp this evening.

30 TH

Our P-38s escorting B-26s to Aversa, Italy, ran into the "first team" of the Luftwaffe, again. This time they were up in greater strength than yesterday. They out numbered our P-38s, substantially. Fifty-plus ME-109s and FW-190s intercepted the formation just after it had crossed the Italian coast. Dogfights took place all over the sky from the coast to the target area and then as far as a hundred miles off the Italian coast on the way back. The enemy was very aggressive, using smart tactics. They would separate one of our flights at a time and go to work on it. A number of P-38s were seen to go in, as were also a number of the enemy planes. One P-38 met an FW-190 in a head-on collision. Both planes exploded in midair. We lost four of our pilots and planes. Lts. Randol, Weinberg, Warmker, and F/O Deisenroth are all missing and were not seen to have come out of the target area. Lt. Warmker was seen to crash in the water after his plane stalled out in a climb. A number of parachutes were seen to open. We had five victories. Lt. Hurst claimed two ME-109s "destroyed," Lt. McIntosh claimed an FW-190 "destroyed." Lts. Husby and Reynolds each claimed a 109 as "destroyed." It was a clear, warm day here at the field. The personnel of the squadron carried on their usual duties.

31ˢᵀ

There was but one early morning air sea mission today. It only got as far as Sidi Ahmed, A/D, where the Catalina they were to have escorted couldn't be found. Today was pay day in the squadron for the officers and enlisted men. Two new pilots were assigned today. They are 2nd Lts. Frederick D. Nichol and Thomas R. Rafael.

WAR DEPARTMENT
A. A. F. Form No. 5
(Revised)

INDIVIDUAL FLIGHT RECORD

NAME LAWSON, Francis R.   MONTH(S) September, 19 43
RANK 2nd Lt., A.C.   GROUP 1st Fighter
AERO. RATINGS Pilot   ORGANIZATION—Assigned 27th Fighter Sq.
TRANSFERRED FROM   ORG.—Attached for flying
TO   DATE   STATION APO # 520

1	2	3	4 PILOT TIME BY AIRPLANE TYPE						5 Aircraft Model Symbol	6 No. of Landings	7 Other Than Pilot	8 REMARKS
Date	Duty	Mission Symbol	Attack	Bomb.	Obs.	Pursuit	Cargo	Training				
1	P	A				1:30			F-39F	1		Mateur-Local
2	P	A				3:00			F-39G	2		" "
3	P	A				1:15			"	1		" "
4	P	A				1:15			"	2		" "
5	P	C				4:15			"	1		Mateur-Naples-Mateur
6	P	C				4:30			"	2		Mateur-Naples-Termini -Gerbini (Sicily)
9	P	C				4:00			"	1		Gerbini-Naples-Ger.
9	P	C				3:00			"	1		" " "
10	P	C				4:15			"	1		Gerbini-Salerno-Ger.
11	P	C				3:15			"	1		Gerbini-Naples-Gerbi
11	P	C				2:45			"	1		" " "
12	P	C				3:15			"	1		Base-Apples-Base
13	P	C				3:00			"	1		Base-Apples-Base
14	P	C				3:00			"	1		" " "
14	P	C				3:00			"	1		" " "
15	P	C				3:00			"	1		" " "
16	P	C				2:30			"	1		" " "
17	P	A				1:00			"	2		Local
20	P	A				1:00			"	2		Local-Mateur
21	P	A				3:30			"	2		Mateur-Algiers-Mat.
24	P	A				1:30			"	1		Mateur-Local
24	P	A				1:45			"	1		" "
25	P	A				0:45			"	1		" "
25	P	A				1:45			"	3		" "
30	P	C				4:00			"	1		Mateur-Italy-Mateur

				9 Total pilot time	10 Total other than pilot	11 Pilot time nonmilitary airplanes	12
TOTALS							
This report			66:00	66:00			
Previous reports this F.Y.			57:50	57:50		55:4	
Totals this fiscal year			123:50	123:50		121:45	
Totals previous years			219:25	219:25			
Totals to date			343:15	343:15			

*DUTY SYMBOLS
P—Pilot   B—Bomber   R—Radio operator
CP—Copilot   OB—Observer   PU—Photographer   **DUPLICATE**
N—Navigator   E—Engineer   O—Other crew
C—Command Pilot   G—Gunner   X—Passenger

NOTE.—When the airplane is assigned to an organization other than that on which the individual is assigned or attached for flying, show the airplane organization under Remarks, column 8.

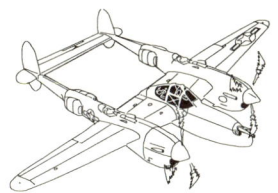

WAR DIARY OF THE 27ᵀᴴ FIGHTER SQUADRON

September 1943

1ST No mission scheduled for today. Lt. Husby, who had landed in Sicily with his damaged plane after yesterday's mission, returned today. He had a number of small shrapnel wounds in his back which required medical attention. Lt. Husby claimed an ME-109 as destroyed in the battle yesterday. Today was somewhat cooler than usual and it was pleasant all day.

2ND Again there was no mission. A number of the new pilots went up before daybreak on a training flight. It was a warm clear day here at the field. A list of the enlisted men who are to go on the advance echelon was posted today. About 65 of them, and three ground officers, are to make the trip. They were all called together this morning and told what preparations to make. About ten of the pilots flew a practice mission after dark tonight.

3RD Another one of those "Scorchers." There was no combat mission today. The pilots have been getting a well-deserved rest these past few days. Some of them spend their time loafing around the camp while others have taken trips into Tunis and other places close by. A false alarm

SEPTEMBER 1943

air-raid routed everyone out of bed just before midnight. Captain Pate is the new group commander, and Captain Newbury succeeds him as our squadron commander. This change was made effective today. The preparations for the move by the advance echelon, are just about complete, and it is expected they will leave in the next day or two.

[Note: The invasion today was an initial landing by the British Eighth Army on the southernmost tip of Italy.]

4 TH As the invasion of the Italian mainland was made yesterday, our brief rest was brought to an end. This afternoon twelve of our planes went out on a fighter sweep to strafe aircraft on the ground at Grazzanise A/D in Italy. About ten miles off the coast of Italy, going in, Lt. Butler, who was leading the squadron, was forced to drop out because of electrical trouble. The rest of the planes continued on into Italy, but had trouble locating their intended target. The weather was very bad, which added to their difficulties. They did, however, strafe a number of targets of opportunity and Lt. Schranz destroyed an FI-156 in the air. The men of the squadron carried on their usual squadron duties. The weather over the field was CAVU [ceiling and visibility unlimited] all day. Captain Pate was elevated to the rank of Major today.

5 TH The first group of thirty-five men left this morning on British transports for the new field in Sicily. Another group left this afternoon. Eighteen of our planes escorted the B-26s to bomb Grazzanise Satellite #1. The results of the bombing were not observed because of intervening clouds. All of our planes returned safely. No enemy aircraft were encountered though about a dozen were called in over the radio. We had another paratroop alert about midnight; the airplane guards had to be doubled. Lt. Butler, who landed in Sicily yesterday, returned this

27TH FIGHTER SQUADRON   SEPTEMBER 1943

afternoon. Second Lt. Nathan Pelcovits was assigned to the squadron today from group headquarters. He is to be Assistant S-2 Officer [Intelligence].

COMMENTS 9/5/43: After six training flights around Mateur, today was my first combat mission. This is the first error that I have found in these daily entries: when the diary reported "No e/a (enemy aircraft) were encountered though about a dozen were called in over the radio." How could I ever forget? My first mission was number II on F/O Styer's wing. I was more afraid of failure than I was of being shot down. Irv Styer was one of the more experienced pilots in the squadron and in his position as squadron leader, number II was the safest spot to be. I had been thoroughly briefed that all I had to do was "stay on his wing - no matter what!" This I did with a vengeance. Irv got in a good long burst on an ME-109 which he claimed destroyed but, with "new guy" on his wing on his first mission, I did not see him go down, so consequently it was not confirmed. I don't think that Irv ever forgave me for that. What he did not know was that I had never seen a P-38 with all five guns blazing and when that erupted from the nose of my leader with a hailstorm of empty casings streaming from underneath I thought, "Oh dear, Irv is getting shot to pieces and I am not even sure where we are!" After the first mission the learning curve was almost vertical. "On the job training" is very effective when success means that you get to do it all over again and failure means that you do not. I was now "IN THE WAR."

6 TH Twenty-one of our P-38s took off from Mateur, North Africa, to escort B-26s bombing Grazzanise A/D, Italy. Due to the heavy overcast, the rendezvous with the B-26s failed, but our planes overtook the bombers before the target was reached. The results of the bombing were not observed. Our P-38s were attacked by twenty ME-109s, MA-200s, and MA-202s. During one engagement with the enemy, 1st Lt. Otto A. Hloucal, Jr., shot down an ME-109. This was the squadron's 100th victory. F/O Stunkard crash-landed at Ponte Oliva, Sicily. He was not injured. This morning the remainder of the men who formed the advance echelon arrived at Dittano, Sicily. Our new field is situated about twenty miles southeast of Mt. Etna. Camp was set up and everything started operating as smooth as ever. Since only a skeleton crew is on hand, each man will be under a bit of pressure for the next few days. The weather is warm and there was a 6/10th overcast throughout most of the day.

Those of us left back at Mateur had quite a bit of excitement this evening in the form of an air raid. While most of the men were attending a movie at Group Headquarters, the enemy started an attack on the harbor at Ferryville. They dropped a number of flares, some of which seemed to be just over the P-40 field on the other side of town. As usual the enemy planes seemed to use a point just over our field to start their bomb run on the harbor. There seemed to be a great number of planes in on the raid which lasted about forty-five minutes. The hardworking Beaufighters [British night fighters] were operating just outside of the target area, and we saw them shoot one of the bandits down less than five miles from our camp. He burst into flames and crashed into the mountain just north of us. We heard later, that three more were shot down that way and another four fell victims to our "Ack-Ack" fire. The raid couldn't have been very successful from Jerry's point of view.

COMMENTS 9/6/43: It is amazing how much one can learn in one day. Of course, starting from zero, even one lesson is a one hundred percent growth. Today was my second mission and, admittedly, I had gained a lot of confidence since yesterday. I was even able to look about in the target area and got off a short burst at one of the ME-109s as he sailed past high overhead. I doubt that he saw the tracers. We landed at our new field in Sicily and, much to my surprise, tents were already set up and some of our bedding and such was on hand. Initially, the airplanes had to be refueled by passing up five gallon cans of gasoline to the crew chief on top of the wing. Counting up how much work that requires (over 400 gallons for each plane), we can appreciate the backbreaking effort that our maintenance people put forth. There were still a few skeletons of German aircraft littered about the field which was nothing more than a flat area between olive and almond groves. Fortunately, this was the dry season because I suspect that with any rain we would have been up to our "knee-bones" in mud.

7TH

There was no combat mission this morning. Most of the day was taken up with practice flights. Everyone is in fine spirits and ready for the big thing that is certain to come off soon. The group and squadron officers were busy getting plans set for the coming event. The weather here was very warm, with a 3/10th overcast over the field. Usual camp duties were performed by the men back at Mateur. The weather continues to be nice. Two more pilots went over to Sicily this morning, and two more enlisted men. All that remained of Lt. Kuba was sent to us today. A burnt identification card, and two burnt letters which had been taken from the ashes of his crashed plane by an Italian officer who was recently taken prisoner by our forces.

8TH

Fifteen of our P-38s kept a vigilant watch over one of our convoys headed towards Naples, Italy, from dawn to dusk. The first plane took off at 0801 hours and the last one was down at 1356 hours. Everyone returned safely to the base. Major General Bissel, formerly one of our air chiefs in India, visited our group headquarters this morning. He was accompanied by Brigadier General Hood and Colonel Kyle, Chief of Staff for the 12th Fighter Command. The weather was 5/10th overcast and very warm during the day.

Back at Mateur we had beer as a treat for this evening. It helped celebrate the news of Italy's capitulation, which we heard of this evening just after supper. Captain Johnson called a formation shortly after that and told us that an unusual situation had arisen out of the surrender. The Italian Air Force—those who could escape from the Germans—were headed with their planes for fields in North Africa. We could expect some of them in at our field, he said. We were to be on the alert for anything that might happen. If any of them were to come in, we were to be prepared to put them up for the night, and maintain a guard over their planes. None came in, however, and we were a little disappointed at missing out on a bit of excitement.

Food (chow) line set up in an olive grove in Sicily. Not like home cooking, but they did the best they could under some very difficult conditions. (Bob Share)

COMMENTS 9/8/43: How much the local farmers knew or cared about the "surrender" I do not know; they seemed friendly enough and, like most of the civilians that I encountered all during the war, their main interest seemed to center on surviving. We did strike up a lively trade of cigarettes for eggs and the local wine. (Certainly not "vintage" but better than nothing.) I was a little puzzled by one old man who repeatedly wished us "Bon Jorno." I wondered if he thought that we were leaving on a "journey" but someone finally explained that was simply the standard greeting, "good day"!

9TH

Thirty-four of our planes took off today to patrol and cover invasion forces south of Naples, Italy. The first flight was up at 0430 hours. Throughout the day, flights took off at about two and a half hour intervals. Everyone came back safely. Every flight returning was questioned many times both officially and unofficially about how the fighting looked over there, and about what progress our troops were making. One pilot, Lt. Eickmann, crashed taking off early this morning when his plane got caught in the prop wash of another aircraft. His plane burned completely, but Lt. Eickmann very luckily escaped injury. Here at Mateur we had an uneventful day. We listened eagerly for the news of our troops who invaded the area south of Naples this morning. We also were anxious to get some news of our gang over in Sicily, for we know that they too were having a busy day.

COMMENTS 9/9/43: Diary entries are necessarily blunt and to the point. Lt. Eickmann's crash sounds like "no big deal." Not so! I was next in line to go but all I could see was a ball of flame in the middle of the runway and as I passed directly over it, I was sure that he had not survived. (But I am ahead of my story.) Having never flown the P-38 at night, I was somewhat slow in finding light switches and, without help from Major Pate (squadron commander), I am sure I would not have made it on time. There were no runway lights; only an anti-aircraft searchlight pointed up vertically at each end of the runway. The runway being that black area in between.

The plan was that we would join up in flight formation after take off. That never happened and after a few circles, we were told to proceed to the target area and join up after daylight. So now there is this young pilot on his third mission heading for the most important event in his life — covering the invasion of Italy. I continued north until flak bursts let me know that I had gone too far and was in fact over Naples (about thirty miles past the Salerno beach head). It was still dark as I turned westward out over the water, just in time to see the entire invasion fleet open fire on the beach. This would have been spectacular in daylight. It was even more so in the dark. At least now I knew where I was and where to go.

In the beach head area I joined up with another P-38 which turned out to be Jim Alford (another former P-40 pilot with no more experience than I had). Together we stayed over the invasion area until another flight relieved us and we returned to base. No enemy fighters had showed up and I felt proud of the fact we had finally done what we were supposed to do. After this, I couldn't help but think that anything to come later would be a "piece of cake."

When I got back to my tent, there sat Lt. Eickmann cracking almonds on a steel helmet and none the worse for his very narrow escape.

After the four-hour mission this morning, I got to do it all over again in the afternoon.

10 TH

Thirty-three of our P-38s were up from Dittaino, Sicily between 0413 hours and 1632 hours to patrol beaches south of Naples protecting our invasion forces. All of our aircraft returned to the base safely. Lt. Gerry crashed on the takeoff this morning. His plane burned and he received minor burns. All the missions today were flown without incident. The weather was warm with a slight overcast at the field today. Everyone back at Mateur is getting a little restless from the inactivity. The B-26, which has been used as a courier plane between here and Sicily, had a busy day, making three round-trips with supplies needed by the gang over there.

COMMENTS 9/10/43: After another predawn take off this morning, I am much more comfortable with this night flying. At least now when I look back along each engine, I know that the cherry red glow of the turbo chargers does not mean it is about to explode and burn. (Someone had to tell me that this was normal.)

Frank Gerry was another of the P-40 pilots who came into the squadron with me and his crash again reflected the lack of experience. He thought that he was joining up on his flight lead in the dark; unfortunately, the red light he saw was on the top of a hill and he hit it on the down slope, which is the only reason that he survived.

The B-26, mentioned in today's entry, was the best thing that happened to us. Capt. Purvis, whom you will remember checked me out in the P-38, had finished his missions and was now the #1 Ace pilot, flying in everything imaginable in the B-26. This was an old "war weary" which we had inherited from one of the bomb groups. After all of the guns had been removed, it could carry quite a load.

(NOTE: Gerry was later shot down and spent the rest of the war as a POW, but he did live through it all.)

Thirty-four of our P-38s took off on patrol over Salerno, Italy, from 0540 hours to 1840 hours. Eight ME-109s and four FW-190s were seen, but not engaged. Eight of our P-38s carried 500-pound bombs. They were ordered to jettison them by the control vessel when bogies were reported in the Peaches area. The bombs were jettisoned from 10,000 feet and destroyed four enemy trucks. There were no other incidents, and all of our planes returned safely to the base. Another extremely hot day here at the field at Mateur. There was not much activity during the day. The men worked on the few planes left here to get them in order as soon as possible because every plane will be needed badly over in Sicily. Once again the fifteen ordnance men were transferred out of the squadron, this time to the 6638th Ordnance Airdrome Service Company.

COMMENTS 9/11/43: One more early take off this morning and then another mission in the late afternoon. Using the two search lights at the ends of the runway proved to be a pretty good aiming point, and the night landing was not nearly as difficult as I had anticipated. (Maybe it was just a growing self confidence.)

We had gotten much more sophisticated now with a "direction center" on board one of the invasion ships off the beach. We each had a "grid map" of the beach area and the direction center assigned targets to us with coordinates that could be located on these maps. It worked pretty well, especially when a unit on the ground needed a little help. The maps were divided into two areas, "Peaches" and "Apples" which simplified target location. We were now loaded with one 500-pound bomb and one 165-gallon drop tank. This reduced the time that could be spent looking for targets, but made us a more effective weapon.

12 TH

Thirty-five of our planes took-off to patrol the Salerno area from 0604 hours to 1840 hours. All of our planes returned safely to the base. The weather continues to be warm, and there was a 3/10th overcast at the field most of the day. The EM working on the line have been doing a very good job keeping the planes in the air. They have had to work very long hours, getting up before dawn and working on the aircraft until after sunset. The meals haven't been the best, but there hasn't been any more than the usual amount of complaints. Ten men were sent to Sicily today to replace a few of the fellows over there. We hear that they have been getting a real workout. This was a warm clear day here at the field at Mateur.

COMMENTS 9/12/43: Only got to fly one mission today. Things have more or less settled into a routine, but each mission always has the "unexpected." The item in the diary entry about the line maintenance people doing such a good job and working long hours can never be overstated. It was nothing short of miraculous when you consider the conditions under which they were working. We do at last have fuel tankers instead of the five-gallon cans that were used at first.

13TH

Eighteen of our P-38s were up from 0557 hours to 1255 hours to patrol over the land forces between Salerno and Naples. All of our aircraft returned to base. No enemy planes were seen. Captain Newbury was promoted to the rank of Major. The usual squadron duties were carried on by the men here at Mateur. The morale is high as always.

COMMENTS 9/13/43: Again I was on the early mission, but it was at least light enough to see the runway. I had mentioned that these diary entries were made by the Intelligence people which is correct for the most part; however, some of these are by our executive officer, Maj. Andy Johnson. He was the "old man" of the squadron, in his late "twenties," and a real stabilizing influence. Squadron commanders and operations officers were all pilots, and they completed a tour (if they survived) and rotated back to the States usually in less than one year. Andy, on the other hand, was not a pilot and had been with the squadron since it came overseas. With the squadron split in two locations, Andy was running the show at Mateur while Major Newbury and the operations officer, Lt. Butler, were taking care of things here in Sicily.

14TH

Thirty-five of our P-38s flew a total of five missions throughout the day. All of them returned safely to the base. One flight, led by Lt. Butler, dive-bombed a railroad junction and destroyed many boxcars, gasoline cars, and the railroad tracks. All of the bombs of the flight resulted in direct hits on the target. Lt. Laird, who was injured in an air battle last month, flew on his first mission since being released from the hospital. The weather was warm with a slight haze over the field.

The men here at Mateur went in trucks to Tunnis this evening to see the Red Cross stage revue, "As You Were." In the cast there were a number of stage girls from Broadway, who drew many an "ooh and an ah" from the audience of Allied servicemen.

COMMENTS 9/14/43: Nothing spectacular on my mission in the morning, but the late afternoon mission was a different story. The direction center sent us into a major rail junction in the town of Avaleno. I was number two on Lt. Butler's wing, and we were each loaded with a 500-pound bomb. There were at least six or eight parallel tracks, each with a long train. Bomb aiming was rather primitive, but effective, in that we lined the target between the two top gun barrels and as it drifted under the nose at about three thousand feet above ground, we released. Looking back as I pulled off the target, the entire rail yard was a mass of flame. One of my proudest moments was when Lt. Butler singled me out at debriefing and excitedly announced, "'Two', your bomb went down the filler cap on a tank car and torched the whole place." (Several months later, while driving to Naples, we went through Avaleno and drove by the rail yard. Numerous tank cars were burned out with the frames literally melted down over the axles.)

15 TH

Thirty-six of our P-38s took off today to dive-bomb targets of opportunity in the Naples area. All of them returned safely to the base. The mission was partially successful. Four ME-109s were seen in the vicinity of the target, but were not engaged. F/O Styer completed his 50th mission today. Major Pate and Lt. Adams flew in the piggyback to Sicily. Major Newbury, taking off at the same time in another piggyback, was forced to turn back because of engine trouble. He took off later in another ship.

COMMENTS 9/15/43: Hard to believe that this morning completed my thirteenth mission. No longer a "new guy," I have graduated to number four (ass end Charlie) and even fly number three (element lead). Experience is relative and the difference between thirteen missions and one or two is quite significant.

The Lt. Adams mentioned in today's entry is Doctor Adams, our squadron flight surgeon. He missed no opportunity to be a part of whatever we were doing. Strangely enough, in his civilian practice he was an obstetrician and now the fortunes of war had him caring for a bunch of fighter pilots and maintenance crews. Doc was quite a man and several chapters could be written about his activities.

16 TH

Thirty-four of our P-38s took-off today to dive-bomb and strafe targets of opportunity in the Naples area. All of our aircraft returned safely to the base. One P-38, Lt. Petersen, crash landed upon returning. His airplane received a 20mm shell in the left wing and several machine gun bullets in the cowling of the left engine which damaged the hydraulic system. Lt. Petersen was bruised rather painfully by the crash.

Jack Benny was making a personal appearance in Tunis this evening, so a truckload of the men went in to see the show. Major Peddie, our new group commander, summoned all the enlisted men up to the headquarters area for a meeting to discuss plans for a club which he suggested. He told what arrangements he had made, including the getting of Italian prisoners to help erect the building. He also has arranged for transportation to Cairo to get the things we need in the way of refreshments. Everyone agreed that this was an excellent gesture on his part and it was also an idea that should have been worked on a long time ago. Plans were made to start work in the morning.

COMMENTS 9/16/43: My flight record shows a 2:30 mission today which is the last one that I flew from Sicily. I do not remember anything spectacular about it.

The entry about the Italian prisoners is not exactly correct. Since Italy had surrendered a few days earlier, they were classified as "co-belligerents." A strange term since they were not Allies, nor were they POWs. Several of these Italians provided some valuable services. One in particular, had worked as a chef in New York, before the war, and he did some remarkable things with SPAM. I have always thought that SPAM got a "bad rap" simply because we had it almost every day for weeks and weeks and no one made an effort to create some variation. This Italian chef, however, did all sorts of things like making up a coating of eggs and flour and even grilling onions with slices of SPAM. It was really very good.

Also, two of these former enemies were skilled carpenters and very good at "improvising." They used "drop tank" crates to construct a lot of items that added to the comfort of our tents, kitchen, and even the new "Club" building.

17 TH

One mission of fourteen P-38s was flown by the squadron today. Their assignment was to dive bomb targets of opportunity as directed by the controller. A railroad bridge was hit. All of our planes returned safely to the base. The weather was warm and clear, making Mt. Etna visible from our camp area.

It was also a warm clear day here at Mateur. The men of the squadron carried on their usual duties. Major Newbury received word this morning that permission had been granted for him to fly his old P-38, "Dear John," back to the States. "Dear John" has really seen some service. It is the only one of the original ships which left the States with the squadron over a year ago, and it is still being used in combat.

COMMENTS 9/17/43: "Dear John" is a familiar term to most in our age group and was widely known as a "get lost" letter from a girl friend back in the States. Whether or not this had any special meaning for Maj. Newbury, I do not know. Majors did not share such stories with second lieutenants, but it was the name painted on the nose of his airplane. I should explain here, that it was a normal practice in most squadrons to assign each airplane to a crew chief and a pilot, with the privilege of having their name painted on it along with some "nose art," if desired. It was also a status symbol to be assigned an airplane, since there were not enough for everyone. You had to work your way up, or live long enough to reach that level.

27TH FIGHTER SQUADRON   SEPTEMBER 1943

18 TH No mission today. All of our pilots and planes and most of the ground personnel returned to Mateur this afternoon. The others will come back tomorrow. They all seem happy to be back, and how they went for the steak and mashed potatoes at noon. After being on a diet of mutton, kidney pudding and tea for almost two weeks, anything would have tasted good. In the twelve days which our planes operated from Sicily, they flew a total of 266 sorties without the loss of a pilot. They surely contributed quite a bit to the successes our forces had in the opening phase of the campaign for Italy. When the going got tough for our troops on the ground the P-38s were sent out to dive-bomb the enemy's communication and transport systems. How effectively they did their job is shown by the fact that after four days the enemy's resistance was broken and our troops were able to forge ahead again.

COMMENTS 9/18/43: Home is a "relative" term and it does not seem likely that returning to the heat and desert of Tunisia would be any improvement over Sicily, but it was home in the sense that everyone was together again and it was a welcome change from the rations so generously provided by the British Eighth Army. (Our base in Sicily was located in the British sector.)

I had now accumulated thirteen missions, which was an extremely rapid and memorable start. Things were about to slow down as we went through several mission changes which would ultimately result in the creation of the 15th Air Force.

19 TH There was no combat mission for the squadron today. The weather was extremely hot all day. The dinner today made one think of a Sunday back at a camp in the States. The cooks went all out to put on a real feed for the fellows returning from Sicily. Most of the men had the afternoon off, as there was to be no flying. Many of them sought relief from the heat by going for a swim in the Sea at Bizerte. Lt. Butler was elevated to the rank of Captain today. Lt. Col. R. B.

SEPTEMBER 1943   **WAR DIARY OF THE**

Richard is our new group commander. He replaces Major Peddie. Major Pate was named Tactical Training Officer for the group.

COMMENTS 9/19/43: Lt. Col. Bob Richard actually joined us in Sicily, but was not designated Group Commander until today. I well remember because I made a fool of myself when instructed to "go wake up Richard and Haynes." Thinking that they were two new pilots, I rather rudely "shook" them awake only to find out later that they were our new group commander and group operations officer. There was never a finer officer and gentleman than Col. Richard. He was greatly respected and admired by everyone. (He survived the war only to be killed in a tragic B-25 training accident while flying as co-pilot with a fellow student at the Air War College in 1948.)

20 TH   No combat mission again today. The weather was very warm, as it has been for the last week. Lt. Gen. Spaatz made a formal presentation of awards to some of the pilots of the group up in the headquarters area this afternoon. The general was accompanied by Major General Doolittle and Brigadier General Webster. The pilots from our squadron who received the awards were: Major Pate and Major Newbury, the Silver Star; Lts. Smith, Smythe, Hurst, McIntosh, Purvis, Captain Butler, and F/O's Styer and Wennergren, the Distinguished Flying Cross.

21 ST   Again no mission. The pilots are enjoying a much deserved rest. Today was one of the hottest days we have had thus far. There wasn't as much as a whisper of a breeze all day. Five of our planes were transferred out of the squadron today. We re hoping they will be replaced by the new P-38 H.

27ᵀᴴ FIGHTER SQUADRON　　　　　　　　**SEPTEMBER 1943**

COMMENTS 9/21/43: My flight log shows a 3:30 flight from Mateur to Algiers and return today. While at the Maison Blanc airport, I ran across one of the pilots who had gone overseas with my brother during the invasion of North Africa the previous November. He was now stationed in Algiers but away on a flight, so I did not get to see him. Maybe some other time.

22 ᴺᴰ A two hour training flight was the extent of the squadron's flying for the day. Another "scorcher" of a day. Just before noon a high wind blew up in the camp area. Lt. Adams and Lt. Peterson, our medical officer and engineering officer, respectively, were raised to the rank of captain today. Shortly after dark, about twenty of the pilots with flashlights and a can of gasoline went on a scorpion hunt through the camp area. The scorpions have been troublesome and a number of the fellows have been bitten by them.

23 ᴿᴰ There was no combat mission, but most of the pilots went up on a local training flight. They practiced high-altitude, formation flying, the kind used in escorting the heavies. The heat continues. We had another windstorm which blew down some of the tents in the area.

24 ᵀᴴ Another local training flight this morning with accent on high-altitude formation work. A company of French actors put on a good show for us down in the group headquarters area this evening. The weather was warm, and the skies were dark and threatening, but no rain came.

SEPTEMBER 1943

25 TH Four of our planes that went out yesterday morning on a special escort mission returned this afternoon. They had escorted a B-17 over to Capaccio, Italy, where they remained all night. This afternoon was especially hot. In the evening a number of the fellows went over to the P-40 field on the other side of town to see a show. It was a very good one put on by a number of stars from the States.

26 TH After months without a drop of rain the spell was finally broken, for this afternoon and throughout most of the night it just poured down rain. Just as expected, it turned the whole area into a sea of mud. It sure brought back memories of Nouvion to see everyone slipping and sloshing along to and from the mess hall. Major Newbury left us this evening. He is returning to the States tomorrow via B-17. He was the last of the original pilots who left with the squadron from Los Angeles to come overseas in May of last year.

27 TH Captain Butler succeeds Major Newbury as the Squadron C.O. We had a big mission scheduled for this morning, but it was called off at the last minute because of the condition of the field. They were to have dive bombed an airfield in Yugoslavia. It would have necessitated a round trip of nearly 1,700 miles. We had another downpour this afternoon, which didn't do the field any good.

28 TH The mission scheduled for today was called off, because of the rain early this morning which continued throughout most of the day. Almost everyone spent the day inside their tents. The morale was good as always. Many a laugh was had at the expense of those unfortunates who failed to keep their feet in the slippery going around the mess hall.

29 TH

A bright sunshine, which continued throughout the day, helped a lot in drying out the field, so that it looks like we may end our inactivity with a mission in the next day or two. The squadron had a treat of beer after supper this evening. Since the time was changed last Sunday morning, and the clock set back an hour, it has been getting dark around 7:00 P.M.

30 TH

Our long period of inactivity, as far as combat missions are concerned, ended today. Twelve of our planes dive-bombed a narrow road north of Naples. They were highly successful in registering six direct hits and four near misses. The road had a lot of strategic value, for by blocking it the enemy lost one means of escape and it leaves them with but a very few others. Today was payday for the squadron. Dues of $5.00 apiece were voluntarily contributed towards membership in the new group enlisted mens' club. About 75% of our men signed up.

COMMENTS 9/30/43: Finally back into the war. There had been very little activity since returning from Sicily. We all felt that every day when we did not fly was just one more day added to the war.

The dive-bombing was a little "tricky" since we could only carry one drop tank (bomb occupied the other side) and we had to use the fuel in each engine. I was thankful for the experience on the Avalino mission since we hit the road in the same lengthwise manner as we had done the railroad marshaling yard during the invasion.

WAR DEPARTMENT
A.A.F Form No. 5
(Revised)

INDIVIDUAL FLIGHT RECORD

NAME LARSON, FRANCIS R.
RANK 2nd Lt., A.C.
AERO. RATINGS Pilot
TRANSFERRED FROM
TO _____ DATE _____

MONTH (S) October , 1943
GROUP 1 t Fighter
ORGANIZATION—Assigned 27th Fighter Sq.
ORG.—Attached for flying
STATION APO # 520

1	2	3	4						5	6	7	8
Date	Duty*	Mission Symbol	PILOT TIME BY AIRPLANE TYPE						Aircraft Model Symbol	No. of Landings	Other Than Pilot	REMARKS
			Attack	Bomb.	Obs.	Pursuit	Cargo	Training				
1	P	A				1:30			F-38G	1		Mateur-Local
3	P	C				4:00			"	1		Mateur-Italy-Mateur
4	P	A				3:15			"	1		Mateur-Tunbut
4	P	A				0:30			"	2		Mateur-Local
12	P	A				3:15			"	1		Mateur-Mateur
16	P	A				1:1			"	1		Mateur-Local
17	P	A				0:30			"	1		Mateur-Bizerte
17	P	A				1:30			"	1		Mateur-Local
17	P	A				1:15			"	1		" "
13	P					1:45			"	1		" "
20	P	C				4:15			"	1		Mateur-Rome-Mateur
7	P	C				2:30			"	1		Tunbut-Cyprus
8	P	A				3:00			"	1		Cyprus-Tunbut
21	X	A							F-38G		1:30	Tunbut-Algiers
22	X	A							"	1	1:25	Algiers-Mateur
22	P	A				1:10			F-38G	1		Mateur-Local
25	P	T				1:30			"	1		Mateur-Local
30	P	A				0:30			"	1		Mateur-Local
31	P	C				4:30			"	1		Mateur-Rome-Mateur

									9	10	11	12
TOTALS									Total pilot time	Total other than pilot	Pilot time nonmilitary airplanes	
This report						41:25			41:25		41:25	
Previous reports this F. Y.						123:50			123:50		121:45	
Totals this fiscal year						165:15			165:15		163:10	
Totals previous years						219:25			219:25			
Totals to date						384:40			384:40			

* DUTY SYMBOLS
P—Pilot B—Bomber R—Radio operator
CP—Copilot OB—Observer PH—Photographer
N—Navigator E—Engineer O—Other crew
C—Command Pilot G—Gunner X—Passenger

NOTE.—When the airplane is assigned to an organization other than that to which the individual is assigned or attached for flying, show the airplane organization under Remarks, column 8.

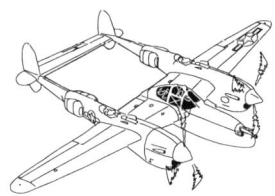

WAR DIARY OF THE 27ᵀᴴ FIGHTER SQUADRON

October 1943

1ST The mission for today was to be a dive-bombing job just as yesterday. Fifteen P-38s, each carrying a thousand-pound bomb, took off at noon to bomb highway bridges over the railroad two miles southeast of Mignamo, Italy. They were unable to locate their target because of the extremely bad weather and poor visibility. All returned safely with their bombs to the base. The weather at the field was likewise poor with threatening clouds hanging low overhead all day. The squadron received official notice from the War Department that 2nd Lt. Thorman R. Neilson, who was lost on a mission over Sardinia in June, is now a prisoner of war in Germany. We also received word from relatives of Captain Theodore H. Runyon, that he too was a prisoner of war in Germany. It is always good to hear that those fellows are at least still alive.

2ND The only activity today was a weather observation and reconnaissance mission. Four of our P-38s escorted a B-26 to the Gulf of Naples. They encountered very poor weather over there just as we had at the field most of the day. We had a rainstorm about mid-afternoon which lasted until late in the evening. The camp area was messed up quite a bit by it.

COMMENTS 10/2/43: I had a 1:30 flight this morning (not a combat mission), probably a local maintenance test flight. By this afternoon a forerunner of wet weather, which was to plague us and eventually drive us from the "dry" lake bed at Mateur, showed up with a vengeance. It is difficult to imagine how the ordinarily simple functions of living are disrupted by such rain storms. However, almost everything we did was necessarily done outdoors; eating, washing, working, and even the "outhouse" was open to the elements.

3RD

Four of our planes managed to get off early this morning to escort a B-26 on another weather observation and reconnaissance mission over the Gulf of Gaita. A bright sunshine all morning helped the condition of the field to such an extent that sixteen of our planes were able to get off just before noon. They went to bomb highway overpasses near Mignamo, Italy. Seven hits or near misses on the passes were observed. No enemy planes were encountered and all of our planes returned safely. Nothing of special interest in the squadron today. The enlisted men carried out their usual squadron duties.

COMMENTS 10/3/43: The fact that we were able to get a combat mission off the ground speaks volumes about the effort of the maintenance people and the ability of the P-38 to lift off a load like we had in all that mud. One of my concerns (trivial though it may seem) was how would we ever get the mud out of the cockpit which had been tracked in on my feet. Maybe it was a holdover from childhood when my mother made us take off our muddy shoes before coming in the house.

We are becoming quite proficient at hitting bridges and roadways. It is amazing what a little practice or experience can do.

At five o'clock this morning the whole camp was awakened and assembled. The names of eighty-two men were called and those men were told to be ready to move in three hours. There was a great deal of activity from then on — everyone wondering where it would be this time. It wasn't until just before taking off that we found out what our destination was to be. I think everyone was a bit disappointed when they heard they were going to a field in Libya, about forty miles east of Tobruk. Transports were loaded and all the men and planes got off before noon. It is thought they will be going to support a possible invasion of Crete and Greece by the Allies. The rest of the squadron is to be left behind, at least temporarily. Twenty-three officers and eighty-two enlisted men made the trip.

COMMENTS 10/4/43: What turned out to be a flight of more than five hours for us in the P-38s was all day and into the night for our crew chiefs and support people in C-47s. Leaving the rain behind to enter the endless blowing sand of the Libyan desert turned out to be "swapping the devil for the witch." The mission was to be escort for British naval ships which were shelling Crete and Rhodes by night, and we were to provide cover during daylight as they withdrew out of range of the Luftwaffe.

By removing the 20MM cannon ammo drum, I was able to bring my folding canvas cot along in the nose of my airplane. I remember that I slept on it under the wing that first night.

5 TH Eighty-two enlisted men and twenty-five officers landed at Gambut #2, in the Libyan desert this morning. Campsite was set up promptly. Water is very scarce here, therefore most of the men remained quite dirty all day. Our evening chow consisted of "C" rations straight from the can.

At Mateur, we had a bad rain storm that continued throughout most of the day leaving the camp area quite a mess by evening. The enlisted mens' club opened tonight. Those who were in attendance— and there was quite a crowd—were pleased at the looks of the place, which was a fitting compliment to those few men who did the work on it. A good time was had by all. The opening was a financial success, too, as shown by a profit of $250.00.

6TH No mission today here at Gambut. The main purpose of this echelon is to operate against the Germans trying to invade one of the Dodecanese Islands. The assignment is to escort some naval warships in these waters, who are shelling the enemy's landing operations. There has been a terrific dust storm most of the day. Sand and dust made up part of the meals today. In the evening, the storm let up a little. Morale of the men was rather low today.

It is difficult to imagine all of the problems that this kind of sandstorm can create. Visibility is down to less than three hundred yards. Camels and Lybian nomads seem to do okay, but this is not for operating a fighter squadron. (Lee)

It was a warm sunny day here at Mateur, which helped to dry up the area a bit. Lt. Purvis took off in the B-26 intending to go to Cairo, stopping off en route at the field where our fellows are with some plane parts and other supplies.

COMMENTS 10/6/43: This was my first experience with a real dust storm. The diary statement that "moral of the men was rather low today" is an understatement. There is no escape or relief; even a cup of drinking water quickly collects a coating of dust on the surface. It is in your eyes, in your ears, in your food and, most of all, seems to go on forever. The British Eighth Army and the German Africa Corps fought and killed each other over this trackless wasteland for more than four years. Looking back on it, how any of them kept their sanity for that long is more than I can understand.

7 TH

Fourteen of our aircraft took off this morning to escort a convoy in the Dodecanese Islands. One P-38 returned early. Thirteen of our planes landed at Nicosia, Cyprus. They are expected to return to Gambut tomorrow. The wind blew most of the day. The dust was so thick you couldn't see your hand in front of you. Another warm bright day. Lt. Purvis returned this evening. He got only as far as our other field. More supplies were needed so he is going to make another trip tomorrow if weather permits. Lts. Hurst, Smith, Smythe, Hloucal, and Schranz left this afternoon. They have been transferred out and are returning to the States.

COMMENTS 10/7/43: As the fourteen aircraft were started, each created its own little dust storm. The desert area was so wide that we all lined up in wingtip (line abreast) formation and took off simultaneously. After staying with the British ships until our relief squadron was inbound, we received instructions to proceed to the island of Cyprus. Visibility was zero at out field at Gambut. About ten minutes after leaving the area, we could hear on the radio what sounded like a huge air battle developing with the 14th Fighter Group which had just relieved us. As it turned out, the Germans sent an entire squadron of STUKAS JU-87s along with one JU-88 (fifteen aircraft in all) out to attack the ships. The 14th Fighter Group destroyed EVERY ONE of them with no losses to the P-38s.

Nicosia Cyprus was largely untouched by the war at that time. Good food, open bars, and friendly people made us feel that we had truly found an oasis from the "Arabian Nights." Dirty and smelly as we were, the local civilians made us welcome.

8TH

Thirteen of our aircraft returned today from Cyprus. Lt. Col. Richard, who led the flight, reported the mission yesterday was flown without incident. All planes returned in good condition. The weather continues to be a nuisance. Dust has gotten into everything. The men were given cots and English desert tents today. This was appreciated by all concerned.

Another warm, bright day here at Mateur, just as it was yesterday. It was uneventful. The men worked on the remaining three planes getting them in order, should they be needed at the other place. Pfc. Wesley F. Bennett was transferred to the squadron today.

9TH

Sixteen of our planes took-off this morning from Gambut to cover a convoy in the Dodecanese Islands. Four of our aircraft returned early because of mechanical failure. Two returned early due to losing the flight in the haze and dust which covered the field. Ten of our planes landed at Duna after the mission, because Gambut was closed in. The field cleared up in the evening and our planes returned to this base. No enemy planes were encountered on the mission. The weather was exceedingly bad today. However, this evening a special service group came to Gambut to show a movie. It almost made this desert seem like a place humans could live in. The film was "The Human Comedy," with Mickey Rooney. It was very good and everyone enjoyed it. Before the picture, Group Chaplain Morford held services.

Back at Mateur we got word this afternoon that the B-26 which Lt. Purvis took off in this morning had cracked up at Bengasi. We did not receive any other details. The motion picture at group headquarters area this evening was the timely "Flying Tigers."

10TH

Here at Gambut we had no mission today. The weather remains as bad as it has been for the past three days.

We at Mateur heard that the crack up yesterday was nothing more than a tire blowing out on takeoff. No one was injured and the plane escaped serious damage. The day was warm and bright here at Mateur. The men carried on their usual squadron duties.

11TH

Still warm, cloudy and dusty here at Gambut. There was no mission flown today.

Here at Mateur we had another warm day. There were threatening clouds overhead all afternoon. Work was started on rearranging the camp area. The tents are to be brought in closer together and lined side by side forming two long rows on either side of the road which is to be used from now on by our vehicles. We have hopes of getting a new generator which will enable us to have a light in each tent. Lt. Purvis returned today by transport.

12TH

There was no mission today from Gambut. The pilots and planes left today to return to Mateur. Some of the enlisted men left this noon.

All of our planes returned here to Mateur this afternoon. The pilots looked tired, their clothes carried a week's desert dust, and they were unshaven. They said they had a rough going in the desert which was obvious by their appearance. They had been allowed only a canteen full of water a day which didn't leave enough to wash with. They say the others will return in a couple of days.

COMMENTS 10/12/43: I am no longer a "teenager"! On this morning, as I was making out the flight log for the return trip to Mateur and wrote in the date, I remembered that yesterday was my 20th birthday. Returning to Mateur from the desert, however, was much more to celebrate.

I am convinced that the four mechanical failures, reported in the diary for October 9th, were the result of prolonged exposure to the dust and sand at Gambut. These kind of problems are to be expected, but hopefully we can get things cleared up soon during some local test and training flights.

13 TH

We had a full and busy day here at Gambut as the men got ready to return to Mateur. There was no mission. The trip to Gambut and back to Mateur was made by transport. It was a long tiresome flight which took approximately nine hours. Stops were made at Bengasi and Tripoli. Some of the enlisted men visited Alexandria, Egypt, before returning to our base at Mateur.

We had a full day of rain here at Mateur. The pilots had a meeting this morning at which each was given a chance to air his views on anything he thought would be helpful to them in future operations. Many mistakes of the past were hashed over and possible remedies were suggested. The men of the squadron couldn't put in much time on the planes today, which are in need of quite a bit of maintenance work after their tour in the desert. Two new pilots, 2nd Lt. James L.

Rodolff and 2nd Lt. William G. Parsons were assigned today. Sgt. Milton Chertock was reassigned to the squadron.

14TH Another bunch of our men came in this evening. Some of them had luckily got a chance to spend a night in Alexandria. They say it is a beautiful place. We had a light rain this afternoon. The men of the squadron carried on their usual duties.

15TH We had a heavy rain this morning that will probably keep the planes on the ground another couple of days. The Red Cross put on a dance for the group in Tunis tonight. About fifty French girls were there and the affair was quite a success. The girls, being greatly outnumbered, got quite a workout. Thirty-six more men returned from Gambut this afternoon.

16TH There was no mission today. A rain, which lasted most of the morning, made the field very muddy. The planes were flown over to Sidi Ahmed at Bizerte this afternoon to get them out of the rain. They would be able to fly a mission from there, tomorrow, should one be called. Five new men were assigned to the squadron today. They are T/Sgt. Paul V. Petuch, Pfc. Richard J. Koos, Pfc. Donald A. Krook, Pfc. Howard M. LaPlant, and Pvt. Edward J. Barrow. Capt. Richardson and Lt. Purvis left this afternoon by transport for Bengasi, where they are going to pick up the B-26 and bring it back.

17TH

With the weather starting to look better, the pilots went by truck over to Sidi Ahmed this morning and brought the planes back. They then flew a practice mission until noon. The new camp setup is beginning to look like something. Lights have been put in all the tents.

COMMENTS 10/17/43: My flight log indicates three different flights today, one being the return trip from Sidi Ahmed (where there is a concrete runway). I cannot remember the other two. The lights in the tents were a welcome addition. Previously we had to depend on candles or a flashlight.

18TH

The combat mission scheduled for today was called off. The day was clear and warm here at the field. Four new pilots joined us today. They are 2nd Lts. Thomas P. Prout, Jr., Thomas E. Maloney, Francis E. Mackel, Joseph P. McGrath. We had an hour band concert at the group this evening before the motion picture, which was "Lady of Burlesque"; both were very good. Another pilot, 2nd Lt. Robert E. Austin, joined us this evening.

COMMENTS 10/18/43: Tom Maloney turned out to be one of the best, and became a very good friend. He served as the assistant operations officer and, later, operations officer. An entire chapter could be written about his accomplishments.

19TH

There was no mission today. The weather continues to be very nice. It was a warm and clear day here at the field all day. The P-47s, which are making their initial appearance in this theater, are based at the former P-40 field on the other side of town. Our pilots, anxious to try out the P-38s against them, engaged the P-47s in a number of dogfights over the field. As so many various conditions enter into it, no definite conclusions could be drawn as to which is the better ship at doing different things. One thing, however, that all seemed to agree on, and that is the P-38 climbs faster. We had some promotions among the pilots today. 2nd Lts. Wingrove, Terry, Tibble, Wellner, and Reynolds were elevated to the rank of 1st Lts.

20 TH To break our long period of inactivity, as far as combat missions go, our planes escorted the B-26s to bomb a railroad bridge twelve miles southeast of Orvieto, Italy. Thirteen of our planes went out, and eleven of them completed the mission. The bombers did not hit their intended target but, instead, bombed an alternate target because of heavy cloud cover over the former. Results were not observed. Our planes did not encounter any opposition and all of them returned safely. The weather continues to be very nice. It was a perfect day here at the field with not a cloud in the sky. This evening the enlisted mens' club opened again after about a week of inactivity. Free beer was on the bill and everyone had an enjoyable evening.

21 ST The mission for our planes was an escort job with the B-26s to Monta Monilno and Marchiano, Italy. Thirteen of our planes went out and eleven completed the mission. One returned early and Lt. Schnurr landed in Sardinia. Six to eight enemy fighters were encountered. Lts. Mc-Quown and Wellner each destroyed an ME-109. The bombers failed to bomb because of the target being totally obscured by clouds. We received nine new enlisted men. They are: Sgt. Abe Fishgold, Sgt. Fred A. Hogan, Pfc. James W. Hamm, Pvts. George H. Clark, Joseph R. Conte, Theodore J. Dobrowolski, Joseph L. Smith, and Bonnie C. Snell.

COMMENTS 10/21/43: Irv Styler and I went to Algiers today in the "piggy back," which is an old F model P-38 with the radios and armor plate removed. Not very comfortable, but another person can fit into the cockpit area. I was able to locate my older brother, who went to North Africa in November 1942 as an A-20 Pilot during the invasion. He is now assigned as a senior staff pilot with Allied Headquarters in Algiers. He was surprised to see me as he did not know that I was overseas. Mail was quite slow.

22 ND Today's mission with B-24s to Turin was called off because of the weather. Late this afternoon four of our pilots went on a Sea Search mission for a dinghy off Cape Biserta. They searched until 6:00 with no results. The weather was very nice over the field today.

23 RD Fourteen of our P-38s went out with the B-26s who were bombing the railroad bridges at Monte Molino and Marsciano, Italy. Our pilots observed ten to fifteen direct hits on the target. Coming out of the target area six or eight ME-109s were encountered. Lt. Wennergren scored a probably destroyed one, Lt. Reynolds damaged another, and Lt. Ferrin scored his first victory when he destroyed an enemy ME-109. The weather was clear and warm over the field. The enlisted men carried on their usual duties. Second Lts. John J. Pegram and Donald H. Colbourn were assigned to the squadron today. Lt. Pegram will be Assistant Adjutant, and Lt. Colbourn is to be our supply officer.

24 TH

The mission today was the same type as yesterday. Fourteen of our planes escorted the B-26s to bomb railroad lines at Terni, Italy. While in the target area our P-38s met with eighteen to twenty ME-109s, FW-190s and MA-202s, who were very aggressive, attacking our formation head on in some cases. In the ensuing "rat race" that followed, and which lasted about fifteen minutes, Lt. McQuown destroyed an MA-202, got credit for a half of a "probably destroyed" ME-109, and he also damaged two more ME-109s. In describing the engagement afterwards, the lieutenant said he had shots at nearly a dozen of the enemy aircraft. He was out of ammunition when he landed. Lt. Wingrove destroyed an ME-109 and damaged an FW-190. Lt. Vondra destroyed an ME-109 and got credit for the other half of a probable with Lt. McQuown. Lt. M. B. Brown damaged another ME-109. On the way home, Lt. Flynn, running low on fuel, landed in Sardinia. In taking off, his nose wheel collapsed when it struck a sand-filled bomb crater. The lieutenant was not injured, but the plane was damaged so bad that it had to be left for repairs. Lt. Flynn returned to the field in a B-26. Lt. Terry had not been seen since the formation was leaving the target area. He may have landed in Sicily or Sardinia. Captain Duke was transferred to 1st Fighter Group Headquarters.

25 TH

Today's mission was called off at the last minute for an unknown reason. The squadron is getting ready to move from here about the end of the week. It is rumored we are going to a field near Cagliari, Sardinia. Most of the squadron will make the trip across the water in LST boats, it is also rumored. Late this evening we had a terrific rain storm which threatened to beat down all the tents in the area. It lasted about an hour and a half. The camp area and the runways were a sea of mud when it finally stopped raining.

26TH October 26th - There was no mission today and it rained almost all afternoon. The preparations for moving continue. The morale of the men of the squadron is excellent as ever.

27TH Captain Richardson and Lt. Purvis returned in the B-26 from their trip to Cairo, Alexandria, and Bengasi. They had a very good time and brought back a number of souvenirs from Egypt. Lt. Terry was dropped from the rolls and listed as missing in action today.

COMMENTS 10/27/43: Among the "souvenirs" brought back from Cairo were several cases of Scotch whiskey. The British always seemed to have a plentiful supply and they were more than generous in sharing it with us "yanks."

28TH October 28th - There was no mission today. The first contingent of men left for Bizerte Harbor this evening. Part of the supplies from each section were shipped ahead. The camp area looks deserted now that most of the tents are down. More of the men will leave tomorrow morning. There will be thirty-five men who will go on the air echelon. It is understood that the air echelon will leave when the other men have reached Sardinia. It rained a great part of the day. Morale of the men was exceptionally high in spite of the food difficulties.

After a day of preparation, the officers and men, who are going by boat, left Mateur at five o'clock this evening and reached the staging area near the docks at Bizerte. The men had to pull out their bedding and sleep as best they could. As it rained, many of them got pretty wet.

29TH

October 29th - There was no mission today. The remainder of the ground echelon left this morning about 0930 hours, leaving the air echelon and flying officers and three ground officers behind at Mateur. The weather again has been a problem. Mud is knee-high throughout the camp area, which consists of three tents. The food situation has been cleared up. The group will have a consolidated mess. Those men going by boat spent the whole day in the staging area, where it rained all morning and most of the afternoon. The area was a sea of mud. A mail call and a movie in the evening did wonders for the morale.

COMMENTS 10/29/43: I am sure that it was not appreciated or understood at the time, however, looking back now, it was nothing short of a miracle that those in charge were able to get anything done. The constant moves, separation of people, weather problems, and transportation difficulties were all minor irritations for a young lieutenant airplane driver. For our logistics people and leaders, it had to be a constant nightmare!

30TH

Fourteen P-38s took off this morning to escort twenty-seven B-24s to Villa Perosa, Italy. The target was obscured by clouds, so Genoa was believed to be bombed. Pilots did not see bombs drop. The mission was one of the longest for our P-38s. They were at 25,000 feet for better than two hours and two pilots suffered frostbitten feet and hands. The pilots were Lt. Wingrove and F/O Morgan. Three of our P-38s landed at Decimomannu, Sardinia, for fuel. The rest of them made it to the base without trouble. The weather was cloudy most of the day with a little rain.

The ground echelon left the staging area this morning just before noon and boarded a British LST boat in the harbor of Bizerte. There were more than a dozen other LSTs lined up taking on troops and

OCTOBER 1943   WAR DIARY OF THE

vehicles. Each one holds a whale of a load. The one our squadron was on had 110 vehicles and 500 men.

COMMENTS 10/30/43: Escort of the B-24s was a forerunner of things to come. While the P-38 was an excellent high altitude airplane, cockpit heat was almost nonexistent. With outside air temperature around minus 40 degrees, it was just not possible to wear enough socks and warm clothing to prevent frostbite.

Typical "Finger Four" flight formation used for most missions. Normally, each squadron put up three or four flights on a mission, depending upon aircraft availability. It is easy to see why P-38s were the most recognizable fighter in the Allied arsenal. (Smithsonian NASM)

Twelve of our P-38s took off to escort B-26s to Anzio, Italy. Our pilots reported that the bombers did an excellent job of bombing. Due to the heavy rain at our base, the P-38s landed at Djedeida A/D. All returned safely there. Fifteen of our enlisted men went to Djedeida this evening by truck. The rest of the men will go there in the morning. We are going to operate from there for a while. Sgt. Bandfield was taken to the hospital this morning. It is believed he has an acute appendectomy. F/O Morgan was also taken to the hospital. He had a high fever. The men of the ground echelon spent the night aboard the LST in the docks at Bizerte. Just at noon the LST moved out into the outer harbor where a convoy was formed and the trip got under way about 2:30 this afternoon. The trip will take about twenty hours, so we should reach our destination tomorrow before noon. The ship rode the sea well, so that there was little roll. None of our men suffered any ill effects this time.

COMMENTS 10/31/43: This has been a "slow" month for me with only four combat missions. Considering all of the moves, I am lucky to have gotten in that many. Today was no exception. When we took off this morning, part of the squadron was at the port in Bizerte, en route to Sardinia, some were still at Mateur to get us off on the mission, and some were at Djedeida to meet us when we returned. Djedeida was located about thirty miles east of Mateur and was one of the very few airfields in this area with hard surface runways. The British RAF owned the field and we shared it with a group of Wellington "Wimpys," twin-engine medium bombers. They operated at night; all night I might add. I asked one of their pilots if they had assigned target times to avoid running into each other over the target. He replied, "No, we all come over the target at the same time from different directions, and at different altitudes to confuse the enemy antiaircraft fire." In amazement, I then asked, "But you have no lights, and exhausts are blacked out; how do you avoid midair collisions?" His answer was a typical British understatement. He said, "Oh I say, you have to keep your bloody eyes open!"

So, we are now operating from Djedeida.

WAR DEPARTMENT
A.A.F Form No. 5
(Revised)

INDIVIDUAL FLIGHT RECORD

NAME LAWSON, FRANCIS R. MONTH(S) November , 19 43
RANK 2nd Lt., A.C. GROUP 1st Fighter
AERO. RATINGS Pilot ORGANIZATION—Assigned 27th Fighter Sq.
TRANSFERRED FROM ORG.—Attached for flying
TO DATE STATION APO # 520

1	2	3	4 PILOT TIME BY AIRPLANE TYPE						5	6	7	8
Date	Duty*	Mission Symbol	Attack	Bomb.	Obs.	Pursuit	Cargo	Training	Aircraft Model Symbol	No. of Landings	Other Than Pilot	REMARKS
2	P	A				1:15			P-38G	1		Djed-Ste. Marie Duzte
3	P	A				1:30			"	2		Ste Marie Duzte-Djed-Ste Marie Duzte
7	P	A				1:30			"	3		Ste Marie Duzte-Djed
10	P	T				3:00			"	1		Djed-Early Return.
11	P	T				1:15			"	1		Djedeida-Local.
13	P	T				2:15			"	1		Djed-Decimo-Djed.
15	P	C				8:45			"	3		Djed-Gerbini-Athens-Lecce-Djedeida.
18	P	T				3:00			"	1		Djed-Sard-Djed.
19	P	A				2:00			"	2		Djed-Elmas-Djed.
24	P	A				2:30			"	2		Djed-Elmas-Djed.
26	P	C				5:30			"	2		Djed-Italy-Djed.

				9	10	11	12
TOTALS				Total pilot time	Total other than pilot	Pilot time nonmilitary airplanes	
This report			32:30	32:30		32:30	
Previous reports this F.Y.			165:15	165:15		163:10	
Totals this fiscal year			197:45	197:45		195:40	
Totals previous years			219:25	219:25			
Totals to date			417:10	417:10			

*DUTY SYMBOLS
P—Pilot B—Bomber R—Radio operator
CP—Copilot OB—Observer PH—Photographer
N—Navigator E—Engineer O—Other crew
C—Command Pilot G—Gunner X—Passenger

NOTE.—When the airplane is assigned to an organization other than that to which the individual is assigned or attached for flying, show the airplane organization under Remarks, column 8.

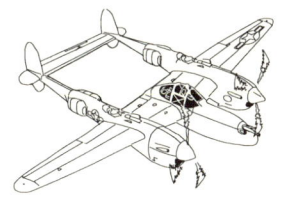

WAR DIARY OF THE 27TH FIGHTER SQUADRON

November 1943

1ST No mission today. This morning all of the tents were taken down. The entire group of men who form the air echelon left Mateur and went to Djedeida. Camp was set up there just after noon. Chow consisted of a cheese sandwich. The evening meal more than made up for it though.

The advance ground echelon arrived at Cagliari, Sardinia, this morning, shortly before noon. The men and vehicles were unloaded by mid-afternoon. Camp for the 27th was set up in a villa about a mile from the airfield and a mile from Cagliari, on the main road leading into the city. It is one of the nicest campsites the squadron has ever had. A two story, pink colored, stone house will serve as Squadron Headquarters building. The house is surrounded by beautiful and well-kept gardens and orchards. There is also a large chapel about a quarter of a mile from the house which some of the men will use as sleeping quarters. Other men have cleaned up the stables and the servants quarters and have moved into them. The rest of the men are in tents on the grounds between the house and the stables.

COMMENTS 11/1/43: Even though it would be several weeks before we joined the rest of the squadron in Sardinia, I made a few ferry flights (taking in mail and such) and remember that everything said about the new camp was true. There was even a multistory building where the pilots of the 27th set up quarters and it was by far the best that I had seen anywhere overseas.

2ND Eleven of our P-38s escorted B-26s to Terni, Italy, where the railroad bridges were bombed. All of our aircraft returned safely to the base. Lt. Charley W. Brown flew his first combat mission since returning to the squadron from the hospital. Lt. Brown sustained injuries when he was shot down over Sicily in July. Lt. Husby finished his 50th combat mission today. The weather at Djedeida was 4/10th overcast and cool. We had no rain for a change. The people here around Cagliari seem to be as bad off as the Arabs were back in Africa. They crowd around our camp area at mealtimes, hoping to get what they can to eat. The fellows were generous, as usual, and gave away a lot of their own rations. The city of Cagliari has been badly blasted by our bombers. Hardly a place has been left untouched. It puts us in mind of Hull, back in England, or Bizerte, over in Africa. Most of the day the men spent fixing up their living quarters. Lights have been put in and everyone is well satisfied with things in general.

3RD No mission today. The weather at Djedeida was cloudy and cool. The men spent a lot of the day pretty close to the "pad."

The men over in Sardinia carried on their usual camp duties. Six Italian civilians were hired to act as KPs and to do general duty about the camp. Until other supplies come in from the mainland, our diet is going to be mostly "C" rations. We had a show over on the airfield in one of the hangers this evening. The hangers still have a number of German and Italian planes in them. We had a heavy rain which lasted most of the night.

27ᵀᴴ FIGHTER SQUADRON   NOVEMBER 1943

COMMENTS 11/3/43: There was an Italian fighter squadron on the airfield and the pilots seemed friendly enough, but I never did figure out what their status or their mission was to be. (I doubt that they knew either.) Their little single-engine fighter, Regiane RE-2000, was probably the cleanest and best looking airplane that I had ever seen. I really wanted to get a flight in one, but of course that was not allowed. The Italians would run the engines up and take the cowling off to work on them, but I never saw one fly. Like the Americans, they had a squadron insignia (a cat with its tail up in a fighting stance); naturally they were known as the "Black Cat Squadron."

4ᵀᴴ Twelve of our P-38s were up this morning on a dive-bombing mission. They were escorted by the 71st and 94th Squadrons. The target was an important viaduct near Terni, Italy. Lt. Wellner led the squadron and reported four direct hits on the viaduct. On his first run, Lt. Wellner could not release his bomb, so he made another pass on the bridge after the last man had finished his run. It was the 50th mission for Lt. Wellner. Lt. Meikle had a close call today. While strafing a train, he came down so low that his petot tube struck a high tension power line, causing damage to his wing and oil line. The weather was very poor today, which made navigating quite a problem. While taxiing, Lt. Reynolds blew a tire and locked wings with Lt. Nichol's plane. No injuries were received by either of the pilots. The men of the squadron over in Sardinia carried on their usual camp duties. A heavy rain, which started in the forenoon, lasted throughout most of the day and night.

5ᵀᴴ The mission for today was called off because of weather. The rain continues to pour down. In Sardinia the men carried on the usual camp duties. A day room was set up in the building, complete with chairs, tables and couches brought in from Cagliari. We had some more rain this evening.

6TH

Twelve of our P-38s were up today to escort the 71st Squadron on a dive-bombing mission near Monte Molino, Italy. The target was a railroad bridge. Three direct hits were observed on the target. All of our aircraft returned. No enemy fighters were observed. The weather was again poor. It was overcast with rains throughout the day.

Here in Sardinia the men are still spending most of their time getting the camp area in shape. The planes aren't expected in for a week yet.

7TH

No mission today. The weather was again very poor. A heavy overcast hung over the field, and a hard rain fell in the afternoon. Most of the pilots went into town, and the men spent their day in the tents close to the "sack." Sgts. Bandfield, Snow, and Babb returned to the squadron after being in the hospital.

Sunday, in Sardinia, the men carried on their usual duties about the camp. A number of the fellows were able to attend church services in the nearby towns. The noon meal of chicken was very good. We had some rain this afternoon.

8TH

No mission today. The weather was very bad. There was a complete overcast and heavy rain at the field most of the day. One year ago today, our advance echelon landed at Arzew for the initial assault on North Africa. Not being combat troops, our echelon followed the "Rangers" in. Then the men hiked seven miles in the cold black night to St. Leu, where they camped until the rest of the squadron joined them the next day.

The usual camp duties were carried on by the men over in Sardinia. Some P-38s passed overhead this morning with a large number of B-24s. We wondered if they were ours. The air raid alarm was sounded four or five times during the day, but no enemy planes were seen.

9TH

Fourteen P-38s took off this morning to escort B-24s bombing a roller bearing factory at Villa Perosa, Italy. Nine of our P-38s returned to the base. Two P-38s, Lt. McGrath's and Lt. Parsons', landed at Ajaccio, Corsica. They both nosed over in landing, but were not injured. Three others had previously returned early. Lt. McQuown finished his 50th mission today. Lt. McQuown has built a good record with our squadron, destroying three enemy planes and damaging several more. He has the Distinguished Flying Cross and the Purple Heart, in addition to his other awards.

The men of the ground echelon here in Sardinia continue to work improving their living quarters and the general appearance of the camp area. Once again, we saw the P-38s go over with the B-24s this morning.

10TH

Eleven P-38s took off this morning to escort B-24s bombing Villa Perosa, Italy, again. The bombing looked good. All of our P-38s got back safely to base. No enemy planes were encountered. One pilot, Lt. Schnurr, was seen to leave the formation near Cape Falcone. His aircraft was found at Decimomannu by a 71st Squadron pilot, who flew it back here to Djedeida. It is believed that Lt. Schnurr was ill and he went over to Monserato, which is nearby, and where the rest of our squadron is stationed. The weather was bad all day. Second Lt.

John W. Campion was assigned to the squadron today. He will be our supply officer, replacing Lt. Colbourn who was transferred out to a replacement center yesterday.

Over here in Sardinia, we are still getting large numbers of the people from the nearby town in our camp area at mealtimes. They wait for what is left over from our chow. The air raid alarm was sounded twice this morning and four times this evening after dark. No enemy planes were seen on any of these occasions. We had rain this afternoon. Lt. Schnurr came in this evening from Decimomannu.

COMMENTS 11/10/43: My flight record shows an "early return" on today's mission. I do not recall the nature of the problem, but I know that I was not flying my airplane "HVA" because I never had an E/R with it. Several weeks before, Lt. Frank McIntosh had returned to the States and I inherited his airplane. T/Sgt. L. E. Olsen was the Crew Chief and, naturally, I thought that he was the best in the Air Corp. We both were proud of the fact that HVA never aborted a mission for mechanical problems.

There were a few air mattresses and sleeping bags, but never enough for everyone. Along with the airplane, I also inherited those two items from Mac. The air mattress had a slow leak, so I had to pump it up every night. Fortunately, it would not go flat until early morning, which served as a built in alarm clock.

No mission today. It was a bright, warm day here at the field. Sgt. Carlton was taken to the hospital this morning. He has the flu. Lt. McGrath, who made a forced landing at Ajaccio, Corsica, the other day, returned to the base today.

The pilots who have finished their missions have come over to Sardinia to join the rest of the squadron. Lt. Purvis, flying the B-26, brought Captain Adams, and Lts. McQuown, Husby, Brown, and

Wennergren over today. Lt. Brown is leaving right away to return to the States. The usual camp duties were carried on by the men of the squadron.

A very proud Second Lieutenant standing beside his newly assigned P-38, 'HVA'.

12TH

No mission today. It rained again most of the afternoon and evening. Lt. Purvis made a trip over from Sardinia this morning in the B-26, and he returned this afternoon taking a load of equipment with him. Lt. Charley W. Brown, who left here yesterday, went to Sardinia, and from there he went to Casablanca. He will wait there for transportation to take him back to the States. While with our squadron, Lt. Brown hung up an enviable record. He destroyed four enemy aircraft.

Two of our planes returning from a mission were forced to land in Corsica. As both of the planes require repairs and servicing, four of our men from here in Sardinia are going up there tomorrow. Flight Officers Stunkard and Morgan joined the squadron here at Monserato this afternoon.

13TH

Twelve P-38s took off this morning to escort B-26s to Istres le Tubes A/D, France, but did not complete the mission. The mission was called off when the fighters reached the point of rendezvous. The bombers were not to be found, so the group leader called the Decimomannu A/D, and was told the mission had been called off. The weather was extremely bad again. It rained and was quite cold.

Over here in Sardinia, it threatened to rain all day, but only a few drops fell this afternoon. A big load of mail this evening did wonders for the morale, as usual. The nights are getting quite cold, so everyone is anxious to see the supplies come in—and especially the stoves.

14TH

No mission today. The weather was rather nice. It did not rain all day. T/Sgt. Olsen and Corp. Jariabko returned from the hospital today. We had a very good meal today, consisting of steak. Everyone was quite pleased. Lt. Purvis took Lee, the little French boy that was with us, to

Algiers today, where he will be put into custody of the French. We all hate to see him go, but he will be much better off in school. Lt. Nichol and Capt. Butler went to Sardinia today. Mail for the officers was brought back, but none for the enlisted men.

The usual duties were carried on by the men of the squadron here at Monserato. As today is Sunday, a number of the men attended church services in town and on the field. It rained this evening.

COMMENTS 11/14/43: I do not recall why Sgt. Olsen had been in the hospital; it was probably with "yellow jaundice," which had become quite common. I do remember, however, that I was very glad to see him return.

The little French boy mentioned in today's entry was an orphan whom Capt. Goebel had "adopted" in the area around Constantine, Algeria. I always thought that his name was spelled "L-E-A," but Lee is probably correct. In any event, he was well liked by all of us in the squadron. Lee was like thousands of civilian casualties in the war and I am sure that it was not legal for us to take him out of Algeria, but Capt. Goebel, like most Americans, was more concerned with his well being than with what was legal. He wanted to bring Lee back to the States with him, but that was not possible with the war and Capt. Goebel's return date being most uncertain. I regret that I never heard what happened to the child after that.

15 TH

Thirteen P-38s escorted B-24s to bomb Eleusis A/D, Athens, Greece. Bomb results were good. Our squadron encountered no enemy aircraft. All of our P-38s returned to base after landing at Lecce, Italy, for fuel. T/Sgt. C. K. Smith went to the hospital today. Weather clear and warm today.

Payday today for the men at Monserato and it is the first one for us in a month and a half. It rained most of the day.

COMMENTS 11/15/43: This was the longest mission of the war for me. We flew from Djedeida to Sicily to refuel and wait for the B-24s to pass overhead. We quickly took off and caught up with them for the long flight to Athens. Most fighter cockpits are cramped for space and the P-38 is no exception. After almost nine hours in that confined position, along with the extreme cold of high altitude, I remember that Sgt. Olsen had to help me stand up when we finally returned. On the way back we flew up alongside one of the B-24s and a waist gunner held up a thermos of coffee as though offering a drink. He then ate a sandwich, laid back and propped his feet up to take a nap. I still would not want to swap places with him!

16 TH

No mission today. The weather was clear and cold. At Monserato it was a damp, cold, dreary day. A group of Italians have been working each day on different cleanup jobs throughout the grounds of the villa. The place is looking better all the time. Capt. Butler, and Lts. Rafeal and Maron flew over from Djedeida this morning and returned this afternoon. They landed on the new runway, but because of the rain this afternoon they had to take off from the grass beside the runway.

17 TH

No mission here at Djedeida.

At Monserato the morning was quite cool but it warmed up after noon. Lt. Peagram picked up a lot of good furniture in town which make good additions to our day room. It rained this evening.

27ᵀᴴ FIGHTER SQUADRON   NOVEMBER 1943

18ᵀᴴ Twelve P-38s took off this morning to escort B-26s. When the P-38s reached the point of rendezvous, they were called by radio and told that the mission was canceled. All of the P-38s returned to base. T/Sgt. Snow went to the hospital today. The weather was cloudy and cold.

Lt. Gerry returned to the squadron at Monserato, after his long stay in the hospital following his crash over in Sicily. Lt. Parsons came down from Corsica, where he has been for the past week after being forced to land there returning from a mission.

19ᵀᴴ Twelve P-38s took off this morning to escort B-26s to France. When the P-38s were airborne, the mission was canceled. The P-38s returned to base. The weather was cloudy and cold.

Here at Monserato we had a cold rain throughout most of the day. A rain over here, however, doesn't mess up the camp area like it did back at Mateur. The runway should be ready in the next few days. The engineers have been working night and day on it. Five new pilots joined us here today. They were assigned to the squadron on the 16th of November. Their names are: 2nd Lts. Arustus T. Einwechter, Robert L. McIntosh, David J. Fischer, Armour C. Miller, and F/O Ronald C. Delaney.

COMMENTS 11/19/43: For the second day in a row, our mission was canceled after we got into the air. This gets to be discouraging, after all of the effort comes to nothing.

On the brighter side, one of the new pilots, who joined us today, is an old friend. Armour Miller and I trained on P-40s together in Florida, but got separated after reaching Casablanca. He asked to borrow twenty dollars because, as he put it, "There is no way that I can get away owing you money, so this will mean that I will catch up with you later." I still remember Miller riding up on top of a truck load of baggage, waving a twenty-dollar bill at me and shouting, "Here's your damn money, Lawson!"

20 TH

Twelve P-38s took off this morning, but returned to base after rendezvousing at Decimomannu. The mission had been canceled. Lt. Parsons, who was forced down at Ajaccio, Corsica, last week, returned to the base, after leaving his damaged plane at Monserato for repairs. Ten enlisted men: T/Sgts. Shiffer, Tanner, Kitchner; S/Sgts. Larsen, Herrington, Akers, Crass; Sgt. Lowe; Cpl. South; and Pvt. O'Meara, returned from the hospital today. Capt. Petersen and Lt. Wingrove also returned to the squadron from the Hospital. All, but Pvt. O'Meara, were flown back to Sardinia by Lt. Purvis in the B-26. The weather was 3/10th overcast and cool.

Another cold and rainy day in Sardinia. We had a very unfortunate accident late this afternoon. Lts. Gerry and Husby, together with Flight Officers Styer and Stunkard, were riding in a vehicle which was struck by a civilian's truck just as they pulled out of the gate at the camp. All of them were badly shaken up. F/O Styer sustained a broken leg and Lt. Gerry a broken arm and other cuts. Lt. Husby had a possible concussion. F/O Stunkard was fortunately not injured, other than a scratched knee. All of them are in the hospital in Cagliari.

COMMENTS 11/20/43: Many years later, Irv Styer corrected the diary entry concerning their accident when he recounted, "We were on the highway to Cagliari, going up a hill when we were hit head on by an Italian Army truck." Irv was crippled permanently from that broken leg, ending a very promising career as a pilot. Frank Gerry, "Mr. Hard Luck," had just recovered from burns received in the crash-landing back in September and now, before returning to flight status, was back in the hospital. As a side note, Gerry eventually got back into the war, only to be shot down and remain a POW for the next eighteen months.

21ST

Twelve P-38s took off from Djedeida this morning to escort B-26s to bomb railroad bridges on Cesano River and at Fano, Italy, on the Adriatic coast. One P-38, Lt. Nichol, returned early. Nine P-38s landed at Decimomannu to refuel, then seven took off for base, where they landed shortly before dark. One P-38, Lt. Meikle, flew straight from Decimomannu without refueling. Lt. Flynn did not return. He was last seen going down with black smoke trailing from his left engine after engaging ME-109s and FW-190s. Lt. Alford, whose ship was badly damaged by enemy aircraft fire, and Lt. Reynolds, remained at Decimomannu. Weather 4/10 overcast and cold. M/Sgt. Raymond Manor went to the hospital with yellow jaundice this morning. It was a rather nice day here at Monserato. The sky was clear and it was warmer than it has been for some time.

22ND

Ten of our P-38s took off this morning to escort B-26s bombing Foligno Marshalling Yards, Italy. All of our aircraft returned without incidents. Lts. Reynolds and Alford returned to base. Lt. Alford left his aircraft at Decimomannu. Lt. Flynn, who was reported missing on 21 November, has been reported safe at Amendola A/D, Italy. The weather was cloudy and cold. The enlisted men carried on their duties as usual.

Here at Monserato, we had one of the coolest days yet. A slight drizzle of rain fell this morning. We received word that a 71st Squadron pilot had returned after escaping from the Germans in Italy. He told quite a story and said that our former pilot F/O Deisenroth was among those who escaped with him, and that F/O Deisenroth was still hiding out in the hills in Northern Italy.

23ʳᵈ No mission this date. Weather overcast and cool. It was cold and damp here at Monserato. The men of the squadron carried on their usual camp duties.

24ᵗʰ No mission today. Second Lt. Rafael was promoted to First Lieutenant.

Another cool day at Monserato. A slight drizzle of rain fell this afternoon. The men of the kitchen spent a full day in preparation for Thanksgiving tomorrow. Rumor has it that turkey will be on the menu. Lt. Pelcovits was promoted to 1st Lt. to rank from November 14th. F/Os Styler and Stunkard were also promoted to 2nd Lts.

COMMENTS 11/24/43: With no mission today, I was lucky enough to get the mail run to Sardinia. Just seeing the place where we will shortly be living is most encouraging. Wish I could have stayed over for Thanksgiving tomorrow.

The term "F/O" needs explaining. For a short time during the war, we had a rank called Flight Officer. This was similar to the Army Warrant Officer. It was not realistic to have a F/O leading a squadron, but that was the highest rank attainable. So, Flight Officers were finally commissioned as Second Lieutenants and could then be promoted as their turn came around.

25ᵗʰ Twelve P-38s were scheduled to take off this morning to escort B-26s to southern France. Seven of our P-38s took off when the mission was canceled.

Today is "Turkey Day," our second overseas. We had a very fine supper of turkey, potatoes, dressing, cranberry jelly, corn, fresh butter, bread, pickles, and coffee. It was a direct contrast to last year's dinner of Spam. Our squadron also had its Thanksgiving Day football classic. The officers vs. enlisted men. The officers won 6-0. A pass from Lt. Wellner to Lt. Rafael made the "6" possible. The lineups were as follows: Lt. Wellner, Goebel, Rafael, Tibble, Maloney, Parsons, and Ferrin; the enlisted men were: Sgts. Smith, R. E. Ladson, Meachem, Schneider, DiLorenzo, Hood and Pvt. O'Meara. Thanksgiving Day for the men in Sardinia was one we won't forget. The cooks, together with Lt. Peagram, the mess officer, really put out to the "nth" degree. Tables were set up in the day-room and in the halls of the building. The meal was served in courses. Turkey and all the trimmings — literally everything from soup to nuts. The feast started at 2:30 in the afternoon and lasted until 5:30. A lot of notches on the belts had been let out by then.

26 TH

Thirteen P-38s took off this morning to escort B-26s to Arezzo, Italy. No bombing was done because a heavy overcast obscured the target. All our planes returned to base. No enemy aircraft were encountered. Sgt. Carlton returned from the hospital. Lt. Flynn, who was reported missing on November 21st, came back to the base today. He has been with the rest of our squadron at Monserato for the past few days. His plane was left at Foggia.

Here in Sardinia, our long awaited supplies and equipment arrived from Africa this morning. Our men spent a full day down at the docks, unloading our things from the boat and putting them on trucks, which took them out to the field. A crew worked all night on it.

27TH

There was no mission for our planes today. The men put in a full day on the planes.

The morning, here at Monserato, was spent getting the equipment sorted out and dispatched to the different departments. Word has it that the planes will be in within the next two days for sure.

28TH

Twelve of our P-38s flew to Salon de Province, France, with the B-26s. The results of the bombing were not observed because of the solid overcast at the target. No enemy planes were encountered, though six ME-109s were sighted flying low on the deck below our formation.

Here at Monserato, the men carried on their usual squadron duties. It was a warm clear day at the field.

29TH

The long-awaited day, when our planes finally came in, arrived. All three squadrons landed this morning. A very unfortunate accident occurred when a 71st Squadron pilot crashed in landing and was killed. He blew a tire, which caused his plane to somersault. Our men from the air echelon also joined us this afternoon. They came in on C-47s. For the first time in over a month, the whole squadron is together.

COMMENTS 11/29/43: Of all time to get sick, this had to be the worst possible! I could not even fly my airplane into Sardinia but instead had to "ride" over on one of the C-47s. Even more regrettable, after only one night in our new quarters I went into the hospital the next day. Like so many others, I now had come down with yellow jaundice. No one seemed to know what caused it, and even worse, how to treat it. The mere thought of food of any kind caused intense nausea. The medics did what they could, but treatment consisted of being quiet in bed for day after day until the swelling of the liver subsided.

Only one incident during that time is worth recounting. The German propaganda broadcasts by "Axis Sally" had been very specific about knowing of our arrival in Sardinia with accompanying threats to "visit" us some dark night. After a week or so in the hospital, the air raid sirens sounded some time in the wee hours. At this same time, the engineers decided to destroy some mines in the harbor area by blowing them up. My worst fear was that my family would be told that I was blown up in a hospital bed. What a way for a fighter pilot to die!

By the time I was released from the hospital, the squadron had moved once again. This time to Geoia del Colle in Southern Italy.

30 TH

No mission was flown today. It was cloudy and cold all day over the field. The different departments have gotten pretty well set up, ready to operate.

WAR DEPARTMENT
A.A.F Form No. 5
(Revised)

INDIVIDUAL FLIGHT RECORD

NAME LAWSON, Francis R.
RANK 2nd Lt., A.C.
AERO. RATINGS Pilot
TRANSFERRED FROM
TO _____ DATE _____

MONTH (S) 1st Fighter December , 19 43
GROUP
ORGANIZATION—Assigned 27th Fighter Squadron
ORG.—Attached for flying APO # 520
STATION

1	2	3	4 PILOT TIME BY AIRPLANE TYPE						5	6	7	8
Date	Duty*	Mission Symbol	Attack	Bomb.	Obs.	Pursuit	Cargo	Training	Aircraft Model Symbol	No. of Landings	Other Than Pilot	REMARKS
17	P	A				0:30			F-38G	1		Monserrato-Local
20	P	A				3:15			"	2		Elmas-Palermo-Gioia
23	P	A				0:45			"	1		Gioia-Local
24	P	A				2:00			"	1		"
25	P	C				5:30			"	1		Gioia-N.Italy-Gioia
29	P	C				3:00			"	1		Gioia-Albania-Gioia

			9 Total pilot time	10 Total other than pilot	11 Pilot time nonmilitary airplanes	12
TOTALS						
This report			15:00		15:00	15:00
Previous reports this F.Y.			197:45		197:45	195:40
Totals this fiscal year			212:45		212:45	210:40
Totals previous years			219:25		219:25	
Totals to date			432:10		432:10	

*DUTY SYMBOLS
P—Pilot B—Bomber R—Radio operator
CP—Copilot OB—Observer PH—Photographer
N—Navigator E—Engineer O—Other crew
C—Command Pilot G—Gunner X—Passenger

NOTE.—When the airplane is assigned to an organization other than that to which the individual is assigned or attached for flying, show the airplane organization under Remarks, column 8.

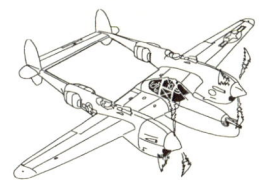

WAR DIARY OF THE 27TH FIGHTER SQUADRON

December 1943

1ST   Starting the nineteenth month overseas off with a bang, our P-38s flew an escort mission to La Spezia, Italy, and got two Jerries. Fourteen to sixteen ME-109s attacked the formation in the target area. Lt. Reynolds disposed of one, and Lt. Ferrin got another. The day wasn't a complete success, as we lost Lt. Vondra on the mission. He was last seen engaging an ME-109. The men of the squadron carried on their usual duties. The weather was somewhat warmer than it has been, and the sky was clear of clouds. Just after our formation had returned from the mission, a lone P-38 came in to land, and in so doing, crashed. The pilot miraculously escaped injury. It was a 14th Group plane.

2ND   Today's mission was an escort job with the B-26s who were bombing the railroad bridges at Arezzo, Italy. Twelve of our planes went out and ten completed the mission. No enemy planes were encountered and all of our planes got back safely. Nothing of special interest took place in the squadron today. The men carried on their usual duties. The weather was again good. The sky was clear and it was as warm as yesterday.

3RD

Twelve of our P-38s escorted the B-26s to bomb Guidonia A/D, Italy. Bombs were not dropped due to the total overcast at the target. No enemy planes were encountered and all of our planes returned safely to the base. The squadron had a big boost in morale in the form of thirty-one bags of packages and mail. Just about everyone "hit." At the field the weather was somewhat cooler with 4/10th overcast.

4TH

No mission today. The weather was a bit cool. The skies were dark and threatening all day. The men of the squadron carried on their usual duties. Today marks our eighteenth month overseas. By way of observance, the new Squadron Club and Bar was opened for the first time tonight. Those few men who did the work of building can be justly proud of their efforts. Sandwiches along with the regular refreshments were served. Everyone had an enjoyable evening.

5TH

There was no combat mission scheduled for today. The new pilots flew a practice flight in the morning. The weather was good. It was quite warm and only a few scattered clouds were in the sky. This afternoon we had a surprise visit from movie actor, Frederick March, and company. They put on an excellent show for us over in the main hanger. Mr. March, getting serious for a moment, gave a very impressive short speech into which he included a message from General Eisenhower. Strong rumor has it that another echelon will leave in the next few days for Italy.

6TH

No mission for today. The weather was cool and the skies were threatening during most of the day.

7TH No mission was flown today. This afternoon General Webster presented a number of our pilots with the Air Medal, Lt. Stunkard with the D.F.C., and M/Sgt. Lang with the Legion of Merit award. The ceremony was held in front of the big Italian hanger on the field. All of the officers and enlisted men of the group were present. Those pilots receiving the Air Medal: Lts. Alford, Eickmann, Ferrin, Maron, Meikle, Rafael, Reynolds, Wellner, Wingrove, Brown, Flynn, Lawson, Nichol, Petersen, L.C., Vondra, Tibble.

8TH Eleven P-38s took off this morning to escort seventy-two B-26s who were to bomb Foligno, Italy. There were no early returns and all of our aircraft returned to Monserato safely. Seventy-four enlisted men and eight officers left Monserato this morning by air transports for Gioia, Italy. Five of the eight transports landed at Gioia and three landed at Catania, Sicily and will join the squadron tomorrow. Tents were put up and general duties were carried out. The weather at Gioia was cool with 7/10th overcast.

9TH No mission today. The three transports that stopped over at Catania yesterday brought the rest of the men into Gioia this morning. Our P-38s also came into Gioia this morning. This airdrome reminds us very much of one in England. The field is a large, flat, green plain. There are British Spitfires and Tomahawks based here also. Our camp area was set up in the south end of the field. Two of our planes had their wings damaged in taxying. Two British aircraft, a Spitfire and a P-40, crash-landed on the field. The pilots escaped injury. The weather was cloudy and cool throughout the entire day.

Back here in Sardinia all but four of our planes left this morning for the new field in Italy. Three of the remaining planes left early this afternoon. One will stay behind here until the necessary repairs are completed on it.

10TH

There was no mission today here at Gioia. The weather was damp and cool, and a few rain drops fell. During the night, a storm descended upon us. There was a very strong wind and the rain came down in torrents. One of the tents in our camp area was blown down. The B-26 left for Sardinia to pick up additional supplies.

Those of us left at Monserato were alerted late in the evening and told to have sidearms readily available at all times from now on. It is rumored that trouble has flared up in the Northern part of the island between Allied troops and Italian paratroopers who are said to be still hostile towards the Allied cause.

11TH

There was no mission today. The men of the squadron carried on their usual camp duties. The weather was cool with a slight drizzle — occasionally the sun would shine. We had rain again during the night.

Usual camp duties for the men at Monserato, the weather was bad all day. A slow steady drizzle fell most of the afternoon and evening.

12TH

The mission scheduled for today was called off. However, a practice mission was flown. The B-26 came back from Sardinia with stoves, mail, and the payroll. All were welcomed enthusiastically by the men of the squadron. The weather is becoming warmer with the sun shining most of the day.

Here in Sardinia we had another cold, damp day with low threatening clouds hanging overhead. Lt. Purvis flew the pilots baggage over to Italy in the B-26 which leads us to believe the move will be more than just temporary, and that we will probably be going to join the rest of the gang soon.

13 TH

The mission for today was called off. Today was payday for the enlisted men of the squadron. Usual duties were carried on. The weather was fairly warm and bright. Towards evening it clouded up and rained a little. Because of the consistent rain, it's quite muddy and wet throughout the area.

Our guess was right it seems—Capt. Johnson called all of us together in the day room at Monserato this evening and told us to get everything ready for a move in the next couple of days. We are going to join the rest of the squadron in Italy, he said.

14 TH

Twelve P-38s took off this morning to escort two groups of B-17s bombing Athens harbor in Greece. There were two early returns, reason for which was the inability to find squadron formation due to overcast. After having been separated from the squadron, two P-38s. Lts. Alford and Austin, landed safely at base. The remaining eight P-38s, unable to locate base due to overcast, landed at Bari where they remained overnight. The weather today was unsettled, partly cloudy, a little rain, and occasional glimpses of the sun.

It rained hard all day and most of the night. By evening the packing of the squadron equipment was just about completed. The men have only to get their personal items together, and that won't require much time.

15TH

Twelve P-38s took off this morning to escort B-17s bombing the marshaling yard at Bolzano, Italy. One P-38, Lt. Fischer, who joined another formation because of a late takeoff, was flying at 27,000 feet when he became groggy due to oxygen system failure. Coming to a 14,000 feet, he flew homeward but landed at Foggia for refueling. Thence, he took off and located base by use of a pocket compass. Lt. Flynn returned early because his fuel pressure was low. All planes returned to base safely, no enemy aircraft having been seen or encountered. The weather today was warmer with 3/10ths overcast.

We had almost a full day of rain. O.D. [olive drab, winter] clothes were issued to the men of the squadron. It was discovered that someone had broken into the supply tent during the night and had stolen a number of things including the personal belongings of three of the men in the hospital. The Italian authorities were notified and they promised to make an investigation.

16TH

No mission today. The weather was clear with the sun shining all day. A chilly wind kept the atmosphere from becoming warm.

It was rumored this afternoon that we were going to make our trip in a liberty ship, but the loading of it was not going to start until Monday the 20th. This evening, however, all the drivers of vehicles were told to be prepared to leave in the morning. Our bar and all the fixtures were sold to another outfit that will be staying here on the Island. We had a nice day as far as weather goes. It even got quite warm this afternoon.

COMMENTS 12/16/43: After more than two weeks in the hospital, I was finally released to rejoin the squadron. Only a small detachment remained in Sardinia, the rest having already moved to Italy. I felt like a lost sheep!

I should mention a comical incident which occurred during my hospital stay. A young Italian girl, who was working as a nurses aid, asked one day, "Tenente, what means the word goose?" Since my Italian was much worse than her English, I tried to give an example along with the definition. "A goose is a large bird, similar to a chicken." A few days later she came in with an amazed expression and said, "Tenete, you no tell me truth. Goose is no similar chicken. Goose is similar injectione!" Obviously some Americano had given her a real "goose."

17TH

There was no mission today. The weather was cool with complete overcast. A little rain fell.

At Monserato all the squadron jeeps and the two command cars were loaded with baggage and equipment and were all ready to leave for the docks just before noon. At the last moment the plans were changed and all the vehicles unloaded. The weather continues to be nice, though it got quite cold this afternoon and evening. A double feature movie was scheduled for tonight over at the hanger but the second film was canceled because of trouble with the P.A. system. Thirty bags of mail and packages this evening did wonders for the morale.

COMMENTS 12/17/43: The last P-38 left behind when the squadron moved was ready to go today and I happily took off for Italy. Immediately after takeoff, one engine overheated badly. The P-38 was powered by two V-12 in-line Allisons which were cooled with liquid glycol. Shutters for each radiator are automatic with an open or closed override. Placing the switch in "open" had no effect. After a few minutes operation above maximum temperature, the engine would usually catch on fire. I do not recall why, but in desperation I moved the switch to the "close" position and the radiator shutter opened! After landing back at the field in Sardinia a simple explanation was found. The coolant switch had been wired up in reverse!

18TH

There was no mission today here at Gioia del Colle. A practice flight was flown, however. The weather was cool and cloudy.

About 1:00 P.M. this afternoon we received word that all of our squadron vehicles were to be loaded on the boat this afternoon. A convoy was formed which then made the short trip from camp to the docks in Cagliari. The drivers had to stand by their vehicles which didn't get loaded until about 9:00 P.M. this evening.

19TH

Fourteen of our P-38s took off this morning to escort back to their base, B-17s bombing Augsburg, Germany. B-17s were escorted safely to Ancona where the P-38s left them. All of our aircraft but one, Lt. McGrath, returned to base without incident. Lt. McGrath was last seen in the vicinity of S. Martine. His aircraft was seen to nose down in a steep glide from 21,000 feet into an overcast. Weather at base was clear and comparatively warm. It was a very lovely day. Much mail was brought in by Lt. Purvis on the B-26. The morale of the men was boosted 100% by letters and packages.

The ground echelon's trip is going to be made on the Liberty ship —the *S.S. William J. Bryan*. It will be our first ride on an American ship. The loading continued all day long. The tents in the camp area were taken down and the men are prepared to board the ship the first thing in the morning. Lts. Tibble and Wellner left us today to go to the 12th Air Force Training Command, and from there they hope to be sent home.

20TH

Fourteen of our aircraft escorted B-17s bombing Athens Eleusis A/D, Greece. Bombing results were good. Five of our P-38s landed at base but the remainder landed at friendly airdromes due to heavy overcast at base. All pilots are accounted for. Lts. Lawson and Peterson joined the squadron today. They have been in the hospital. Weather: cold and 10/10ths overcast ceiling about 400 feet.

Three officers and one hundred fifty-eight enlisted men left our camp at Monserato just before noon and went by trucks to the docks. From noon until 7:00 P.M. this evening the men of the group stood on the docks waiting to go aboard ship. The last two hours were spent in a pouring rain. Everyone bunked up as best they could on the decks and in the parts of the holds which weren't filled. The ship spent the night in the harbor of Cagliari.

COMMENTS 12/20/43: Finally completed the flight from Sardina to Gioia del Colle today. The airfield is a beautiful wide area of green grass. Nice to look at but slick as greased glass when wet. After touch down the airplane was slipping and sliding so that I was unable to stop it, but finally got it turned around and sliding backwards toward the end of the field. Slowly advancing power, it came to a stop. (Probably the first use of reverse thrust in history.)

The pilots were all quartered in an old wooden barracks (more like stables). It was great to be back with everyone but twenty-five or more people in one room and all on different schedules was a bit too much "togetherness."

The previously mentioned British Spitfire and P-40 squadrons were actually South African. They were extremely hospitable and generous in sharing their Scotch with us. I have never known a more rowdy bunch who never wanted to give up, insisting that "you can't quit now, the Queen is awake."

21ST

No mission today. Weather: overcast, heavy and damp. Lts. Flynn, Fischer, Alford, Brown, and Prout returned to base this morning. Reports were received that Lt. Mackle had not landed at S. Pancrazio as previously reported. His wrecked aircraft and remains were found near Mottola, Italy, this afternoon.

The *William J. Bryan* pulled out of the harbor at 9:00 A.M. this morning and our trip began. The ship is very crowded. No hot meals are being served, though hot coffee was put out to go with the cold C rations. The trip was uneventful, the sea was calm throughout the whole day and night.

22 ND No mission. Weather cloudy and cold. Regular squadron duties were carried out by EM personnel.

We arrived in the harbor at Naples, Italy, this morning about nine o'clock. Land had been sighted shortly after daybreak. Shortly afterwards we passed the Isle of Capri—made famous by the song of an American writer some years ago. It rained hard almost all day. We remained in the outer harbor the rest of the day and all night. Naples harbor is one of the largest in the world, which makes it understandable why the Allies stressed so the importance of its capture. We were surprised to see how the area around the docks was lighted up. It prompted some of the fellows to remark, "I'll bet they have a better blackout in New York than they have here only 35 miles from the front lines."

23 RD No mission. Weather cold and damp. It rained most of the day. Pfc. Krook went to the hospital today. Lt. Rafael, operations officer, was taken to the hospital today. Usual camp duties were carried out.

Our ship didn't pull up to a dock until just before dark this afternoon. Two officers and 139 enlisted men got off the boat at 7:00 P.M. this evening and went by truck to the staging area which turned out to be in the buildings of the College of Constanza Ciano on the other side of Naples in the town of Bagnoli. It rained hard all evening, which didn't make the trip any too pleasant. The men who remained on the shop are going to care for the unloading of equipment and vehicles.

24 TH

No mission today. The weather was 3/10th overcast and much warmer than it has been. Some of the men celebrated respectably in their own camp sites and everyone had a good time. Usual camp duties were carried on by the men of the squadron.

Christmas Eve—our second overseas—was a little more pleasant than it was last year over in Africa. During the day, a number of the men got a look at the city of Naples. It is a crowded place these days. Men and women, wearing the uniforms of almost all of the allied nations, were seen on the streets. Christmas will be just another day for the people of this war weary city. A few of our fellows visited the Red Cross Club there. They told of the beautifully decorated tree in the lobby of the building. American W.A.C.s sang carols to the accompaniment of an Italian string orchestra. They said it was very impressive.

25 TH

Ten of our P-38s celebrated Christmas Day by escorting B-17s bombing the marshaling yard at Udine, Italy. All of our pilots returned from the mission to enjoy their turkey dinner. The enlisted men also had a dinner of turkey, dressing, mashed potatoes, fruit, and nuts. The weather was partly clear in the morning but turned cold in the afternoon with a complete overcast. Lt. Rafael returned from the hospital today.

The men of our squadron who were at the staging area at Bagnoli had a Christmas dinner of C rations and most of them spent the day unloading mail at the APO in Naples. Those men who remained on the boat were a little more fortunate. The Merchant seamen were kind enough to share their dinner of boiled ham with them. All of our vehicles got off the boat today and formed a convoy on the docks where they and their drivers spent the night.

COMMENTS 12/25/43: It almost seems unreal that we flew escort for a bombing mission on Christmas Day. However, war is no respecter of calendar or season. After five and a half hours, mostly above twenty thousand feet, it was a welcome treat to return to a real Christmas dinner. Again, I am amazed at the logistic support that enables us to eat in this manner.

This was our first experience with Italian latrines (toilets). They consist of a concrete pad, sloped to the center in which there is a drain of some three or four inches in diameter. Two raised pads (about the size of a brick) are placed on either side of the drain. The idea is to stand on these pads and hit the drain hole! Difficult at best and impossible under some conditions. So much for "old world" conveniences!

26 TH

No mission today. The weather was cold and rainy. Regular duties were carried out and the rest of the day was spent pretty close to the pad.

The vehicles moved from the docks to the staging area. The whole group is going to be ready to take off in the morning for our field which is rumored to be over on the Adriatic coast.

27 TH

No mission today. The weather has been cold and wet. It rained or snowed most of the day. Lt. Goebel was promoted to Captain, to rank from December 16.

At 8:00 this morning our big convoy formed and started off on the trip to Foggia for it is on one of the Foggia airdromes we are going to be stationed. One officer and thirty enlisted men were left behind to care for our equipment still at the docks. The trip was made without incident. We got to see quite a bit of the country and we passed through a number of the towns in which the fighting took place. The Germans had blown up a number of the bridges we had to pass over. The temporary affairs that had to be built to replace them were often only wide enough for one car to cross at a time. That slowed us up quite a bit. It got very cold about the time we reached Foggia and it started to rain. A strong wind topped things off. We had to pitch our tents in the darkness on Foggia #3. There were a lot of fellows glad to hit the sack tonight.

28 TH

Nine of our P-38s escorted B-17s bombing Rimini, Italy. The target was the marshaling yard. All but F/O Morgan returned to base. He landed at Amendola. It rained most of the day and was quite cold.

It remained quite cold all day. Our kitchen truck had broken down somewhere along the way yesterday and as yet has not caught up with us, so we have had nothing but cold C rations.

29 TH

Ten P-38s were up this morning on a secret mission on the Adriatic Sea. All P-38s returned safely to base. Weather was very poor again. Rain and more rain and cold. Regular duties were carried out by the enlisted personnel.

Usual camp duties here at Foggia. It remained very cold all day today. The tents are none too comfortable without stoves which have not arrived yet. No word from our kitchen truck yet either.

COMMENTS 12/29/43: I was fortunate to be on the most unusual mission this morning. Absolute secrecy was imposed, even to the point that we could not discuss it after we returned with those who did not go. Several weeks previously, a C-47 transport with a group of Army Nurses on board became lost due to weather and overflew Bari, Italy, to crash land in Albania. They were picked up by some people friendly to the Allies who moved them and hid them awaiting rescue. This was an elaborate attempt to bring them back using a British "Wimpy" bomber carrying a load of heavily armed commandos, which my squadron escorted. The Wimpy was to land on a predetermined abandoned airfield and secure the perimeter with its forward and rear gun turrets each containing four thirty-caliber machine guns. My squadron was to keep any vehicular traffic away from the field.

The 94th squadron was to strafe the only German airfield in the area to prevent any air interference. The 71st squadron escorted two C-47 transports which were to land after the field was secure and pick up the Nurses.

This was not to be! The Germans had found out about the attempted rescue and when the Wimpy made a low pass over the field, several German tanks were seen hidden under some trees on the edge of the landing area. The mission Commander on board the Wimpy knew that we were very much "out-gunned" so he fired a red flare which was the signal to abort the pick up. The tanks would have made short work of anyone attempting to land or take off. We were all saddened to have to leave them.

Only years after the war, I read an account written by one of the nurses in a magazine (Saturday Evening Post, I think) in which she told of seeing all of this take place from some distance away and knowing that the rescue had failed. She wrote that they all sat down and cried! Happily, they were rescued some time later in a "pick up" from the sea by the British Navy and returned to Italy.

30 ᵀᴴ

Eleven P-38s escorted B-17s to Verona, Italy, today. All returned safely to base. Lt. Austin received quite a scare when the right supercharger in his P-38 exploded. He was near the target at that time. Latest news from the ground echelon is that they have reached our new base and have started to set up camp. Corporal Shores drove the ambulance from that field to this base. Weather dreary and wet.

Two of the cooks hitchhiked in today to say that their truck was seventy miles back, so a truck was sent out to pull it in. The weather remains cold. There hasn't been much activity about the camp area. Most of the fellows have been staying in the shelter of their tents. The wind which blows across these plains is really sharp.

COMMENTS 12/30/43: There is no doubt that some would be critical of the P-38 for what may seem a weakness in superchargers. I do not share that view. Every B-17 and B-24 built during the war was equipped with four, exhaust driven, turbo superchargers. Likewise every P-47 had one, every P-38 had two, and every B-29 had eight. Most of these units were manufactured by General Electric. Turbo superchargers operated at very high temperature and very high RPM. I have already related how those on a P-38 glowed a bright red in the dark. With well over a hundred thousand turbos in service, I am amazed that we had so few failures. Frankly, the turbo supercharger was the "guts" of the P-38 and other airplanes being able to operate above 15,000 feet.

No mission today; 1943 left us in a rain storm. It was a very wet way for the old year to leave us. Many of the men celebrated the old year leaving us in the manner becoming a soldier. Morale of the men was quite "high."

Our kitchen came in this morning and got set up in a hurry, so that we had our first warm meal late this afternoon. We had a heavy rain and a strong wind most of the night which threatened to beat down all the tents in the area. Three or four tents did go down much to the displeasure of their occupants. Capt. Richardson, and the thirty men who had stayed at Naples, came in this morning bringing with them the remainder of our equipment.

WAR DEPARTMENT
A.A.F Form No. 5
(Revised)

INDIVIDUAL FLIGHT RECORD

NAME **LAWSON, Francis R.**
RANK **2nd Lt., A.C.**
AERO. RATINGS **Pilot**
TRANSFERRED FROM _____ TO _____ DATE _____

MONTH (S) **January**, 19**44**
GROUP **1st Fighter Group**
ORGANIZATION—Assigned **27th Fighter Squadron**
ORG.—Attached for flying _____
STATION **APO # 520**

1	2	3	4 PILOT TIME BY AIRPLANE TYPE						5	6	7	8
Date	Duty	Mission Symbol	Attack	Bomb.	Obs.	Pursuit	Cargo	Training	Aircraft Model Symbol	No. of Landings	Other Than Pilot	REMARKS
3	P	C				6:00			P-38G	1		Gioia-Turin-Sardinia
5	P	A				2:00			"	1		Sardinia-Gioia
5	P	A				1:45			"	1		Gioia-Gioia
6	P	A				1:15			"	1		Gioia-Local
7	P	C				4:45			"	1		" "
8	P	A				1:15			"	1		Gioia-Gioia-Gioia
10	P	A				1:30			"	2		Gioia-Foggia
12	P	L				1:30			"	1		Foggia-Local
15	P	C				3:45			"	1		Foggia-Rome-Foggia
19	P	A				1:30			P-38F	3		Foggia-Gioia-Bari-Foggia
21	P	C				5:00			P-38G	1		Foggia-Marseilles-Sardinia
21	P	A				2:00			"	1		Sardinia-Foggia
23	P	C				2:00			"	1		Foggia-Terni-Foggia
28	P	C				4:00			"	1		Foggia-Venice-Foggia
29	P	A				0:50			P-38F	1		Foggia-Local
Oct 23	P	C				5:15			P-38G	1		Mateur-Italy-Mateur; (This Form #1 was lost and the time was not recorded on October's Form #5. The error was just discovered this month.)
29	P	A				0:25			P-38F	1		Foggia-Local
31	P	C				4:45			P-38G	1		Foggia-Klagenfurt-Fog

	9	10	11	12
TOTALS	Total pilot time	Total other than pilot	Pilot time on military airplanes	
This report	49:30		49:30	
Previous re-ports this F. Y.	212:45		210:40	
Totals this fiscal year	262:15		260:10	
Totals previous years	40:35 26:05 231:00	297:40	14:45	
Totals to date	302:50 26:05 231:00	559:55	14:45	

DUTY SYMBOLS
P—Pilot B—Bomber R—Radio operator
CP—Copilot OB—Observer PH—Photographer
N—Navigator E—Engineer O—Other crew
C—Command Pilot G—Gunner X—Passenger

NOTE.—When the airplane is assigned to an organization other than that to which the individual is assigned or attached for flying, show the airplane organization under Remarks, column 8.

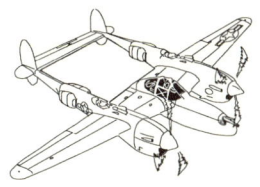

WAR DIARY OF THE 27ᵀᴴ FIGHTER SQUADRON

January 1944

1ST No mission today. Weather was wet, muddy and very cold. Two meals were served today instead of the usual three. The noon meal was held off until three o'clock. We had turkey and all the trimmings.

For us here at Foggia, New Year's Day meant a very good turkey dinner at noon. The camp area is almost entirely under water after last night's hard rain. It got very cold around nightfall. Most of the men spent the day unloading equipment and sorting it our by departments. This field, Foggia #3, is the same one over which Lt. Marcel J. Williams of our squadron bailed out after being hit by enemy flak on August 25th. On that historic day, our outfit destroyed five planes on the ground at this field, and nineteen on Foggia #1.

2ND No mission here at Gioia. It was a bright sunny day. Today is the warmest it has been since we arrived here. The men on the line busied themselves as usual by keeping the planes in condition.

There was a rush to get the stoves that came in at Foggia. When they were set up they really felt good. Usual camp duties were carried on by the men of the squadron. This was another cold, dreary day.

3RD

Twelve P-38s escorted B-17s bombing Turin M/Y, Italy. The results of the bombing were reported as being good. Ten of our planes returned to this field after the mission and the other two landed at Cagliari, Sardinia. The trip our planes made today was one of the longest our fighters have ever made on a combat mission. They covered almost a thousand miles. Corporal Dewart drove down from Foggia, where the ground echelon is, this afternoon. He will pick up some equipment and return to Foggia Tomorrow.

The B-25 group which has been here at Foggia #3 is moving out and they started tearing down their places this morning. Our fellows were on hand early to gather whatever they left behind in the way of lumber, stoves, or anything that could be used for fuel.

COMMENTS 1/3/44: This was indeed a long mission! My flight record shows six hours on the combat mission followed by two more (non-combat) hours on the return from Sardinia. I do not remember who the other pilot was who landed in Sardinia but I am amazed at the correlation between the diary entries and my flight record. Considering the time spent in weaving back and forth over the bomber stream, I am sure that the distance covered would be more than 1200 miles. At the risk of upsetting some of my B-24 friends, I must admit that the B-17s flew a much closer formation and therefore easier to cover than were the B-24s.

4TH

Eight P-38s were up this morning to escort B-17s to Sofia, Bulgaria. Results of bombing were not observed. Three of our pilots, flying 94th planes, returned early because of mechanical difficulties. One of the pilots, Lt. Maloney, crash landed on the field. He was not injured. The rest of our squadron returned safely. Weather clear and warmer although a heavy wind was blowing. Lt. Miller returned from Sardinia today on a B-17.

Today was the first really nice day we have had at Foggia. It was actually warm this afternoon. Most of the men of the squadron busied themselves weatherproofing their tents in one way or another or in putting floors of wood or bricks in the tents.

No mission today. It has been raining all day and is very cold. First Sgt. Selogie and Corp. Dewart drove to Foggia with equipment and returned this evening with mail for the air echelon.

Today, Just as yesterday, was a very nice day. A warm sun stayed out throughout the morning and most of the afternoon. Lt. Campion rejoined the squadron here at Foggia after his long stay in the hospital. Pfc. Krook returned from the hospital, also.

There was no mission today. Lt. McIntosh returned from Sardinia after the P-38 was repaired. Engine trouble had caused him to land there on the 3rd of the month. The weather was fairly clear but still quite cold. The rain has stopped.

Early this morning a strong wind and a hard rain, which lasted until nearly noon, blew down a couple of the tents and made the area a sea of mud. Again everyone was forced to stay in the shelter of their tents. It got really cold late tonight. During the night one of the tents in the area caught fire and burned down. All but one of the fellows luckily got his personal belongings out in time.

7TH

Eight P-38s escorted B-17s bombing a Messerschmidt plant at Wiener Neustadt. There were four early returns. One early return, Lt. Rafael, on the way to base sighted and strafed a German convoy causing confusion and casualties. Results of bombing were not observed. One P-38 piloted by Lt. Rodolff was hit in the right prop by flak which was intense. The remaining four P-38s returned safely to base. Weather was cool.

Usual camp duties by the men of the squadron at Foggia.

COMMENTS 1/7/44: It is obvious from the numbers of aircraft on this mission that we are in serious condition for planes. Four out of eight is also the highest "E/R" that we have had. The maintenance people were pushed to the limit just to get this many up. The intense cold of high altitude continues to be a problem for pilots as well as machines.

The entry about Lt. Rodolff being hit in the prop by flak reminds me of an experience that I failed to comment on while we were still flying out of Africa. I also was hit by one piece of shrapnel which severed the main conduit to the left prop. It immediately went toward low pitch and I could not "feather" it. With the throttle just above idle on that engine, RPM was just below the maximum allowed. The point of this commentary is that even with this handicap, my airplane was able to keep up with the rest of the squadron for the remaining 300 or so miles back to Mateur.

No mission. The men of the squadron were awakened early and spent the morning preparing to depart for Foggia. The trip by trucks was a little cold and tiresome though otherwise uneventful except for the fact that a few of the trucks became separated from the convoy and arrived hours late.

This morning a warm sun dried up the camp area a bit. Those planes of ours which were in commission flew up this morning to Foggia.

Part of the enlisted men came in by truck this evening. The rest will come tomorrow, they say.

COMMENTS 1/8/44: My airplane was one of the few in commission that we could fly to Foggia. Even though this is back to the tents, it is a big improvement over the living conditions at Gioia. The tents have wood floors and a frame with the canvas stretched over it. There are only four of us in each tent and the stoves make it warm enough. The main concern at this point is getting enough airplanes so that we can put up a full squadron of twelve to sixteen on each mission.

9TH Usual camp duties. The weather was very nice. The skies were clear and a warm sun shone throughout most of the day. The rest of the men from Gioia reached Foggia early this evening. Ten men were left behind to take care of our planes which had to be left behind for repairs.

10TH No mission was flown today. A few of the pilots took ships up on local test hops. We had another nice day. This weather is beginning to look more like that of the "Sunny Italy" we read of in the travelogues.

11TH Today's mission for our P-38s was an escort job for the B-17s bombing Piraeus Harbor, Athens, Greece. Nine of our planes made the trip and all but F/O Delaney returned safely to our base. Twenty to twenty-five FW-190s attacked the formation just before it entered the target area. Lt. Maron destroyed one, and Lt. Rafael probably destroyed another. F/O Delaney was last seen lagging after the first break and was not seen with the formation later. Three new pilots: 2nd Lts. Harold F. Lindhurst, John H. Price, Harold M. Lienau, joined our squadron this evening. Lt. Laird, who has been with the 15th A. F. Weather Observation Detachment since we left Mateur, is back with us again.

12 TH A bright, sunshiny day with not a cloud in the sky. F/O Delaney landed at our base this morning. He had stayed overnight at Crotone A/D, Italy. He said he lost the formation when he blacked-out in a break due to insufficient oxygen. About a half dozen P-47s performed over the field this afternoon at a very high altitude which caused them to cut very distinct vapor trails in the sky. It looked as though they were sky-writing.

13 TH Today's mission for eight of our P.38s was to escort B-17s bombing Rome/Centocelle A/B, Italy. Fifteen enemy aircraft were seen in and around the target area, but none attacked our formation. All of our planes returned safely to the base. It was a warm, bright day at the field. There was a 3/10 cloud cover overhead. Pfc. Zalenski was transferred to the 71st Squadron today.

14 TH There was no mission for our squadron today. The pilots had the day off. A few of them went up on local test hops. Another warm, bright day here at the field. There wasn't a cloud in the sky.

15 TH Today the spell of good weather, which we have enjoyed for the past few days, was broken. It was cold and the skies were dark and threatening till about noon when the ceiling lifted and the sun came out.

Our planes went with the B-17s to Arrezzo, Italy. No enemy aircraft were encountered. All of our planes returned safely. Three more new pilots joined us this evening. They are: 2nd Lts. Kenneth E. Hartwig, Robert C. Burgoyne, and Richard A. Cooley.

COMMENTS 1/15/44: my flight record shows "Rome" but the diary indicates an escort mission to "Arrezzo." I believe the diary is correct because Arrezzo is a junction on the main north/south road and railway line about one hundred miles north of Rome. Still unable to put up a full strength squadron.

16 TH

Our P-38s escorted the B-17s bombing Klagenfurt, Austria. Eight of the planes completed the mission. Two returned early because of mechanical trouble. One of those returning early, Lt. McIntosh, sighted a submarine which he forced to crash dive. There were no encounters with enemy planes and all of ours came back safely. The weather was cool and there was a low 6/10 cloud cover over the field. Captain Johnson, our Executive Officer, was promoted to Major effective December 28, 1943.

17 TH

No mission for our pilots today. The 94th Squadron flew our planes on the mission to the Florence area with the B-17s. There was a 7/10 cloud cover at the field. It was cold all day and this evening a very sharp wind blew through the camp area. We had an air-raid alert about 10:00 P.M., but no enemy planes were seen or heard. The group shower—a very sharp affair, rigged up by using an old Italian steam engine and an Italian water trailer—had its opening this morning.

18TH Our P-38s escorted B-17s bombing RR targets at Certaldo, Poggibonsi and other RR junctions in the Florence area, Italy. All of our eight planes who made the mission returned safely to base. No flack or enemy aircraft were encountered. The bombers were seen to hit scattered railroad targets in the area. It was a bright, sunshiny day at the field with a 6/10 cloud cover overhead. T/Sgt. Scoby returned to the squadron after his long stay in the hospital. A large mess hall is being built in our camp area by the men of the squadron. The wood used in the building is from belly tank crates.

19TH This morning eight of our P-38s escorted B-17s to bomb Ciampino and Centocelle A/Ds, Rome, Italy. Six planes completed the mission, the other two returned early because of mechanical difficulties. No enemy planes were encountered. At the field it was a rather cool, bright day. There wasn't a cloud in the sky. The men of the squadron carried on their usual duties. Morale was high as always. Lt. Schnurr is back after a long stay in the hospital.

20TH Our planes did not go on a mission today. The pilots had their pictures taken this morning by the Wing Public Relations Officer. Chaplain Morford and Captain Adams, our Medical Officer, spoke to the men of the squadron who were assembled right after lunch. It was a cold day here at the field. The sky was clear of clouds, however.

21ST Ten of our P-38s went up early this morning to escort B-17s to bomb Salon de Provence A/D, France. Over the target they were attacked by ten to fifteen ME-109s and FW-190s. In the ensuing engagement which lasted about thirty minutes, Lt. Meikle and Lt. Lawson each damaged an ME-109. Lt. Lawson's plane was damaged when a cannon shell burst in the cowling in front of the windshield. He was uninjured and was able to fly his plane back. Four of our other planes did not get back but it is thought that three of them are down at friendly airdromes in Sardinia or Corsica. The pilots still missing are Lts. Rodolff, McIntosh, Fischer, and Austin. Nothing of special interest happened in the squadron today. It was bright and warm here at the field with only scattered clouds overhead. Captain Butler, Lts. Maron, Ferrin, Flynn, and Maloney left today on a secret mission. They went by transport.

COMMENTS 1/21/44: I was only able to claim a "damaged" today because I did not see the ME-109 go down; could not afford the luxury of watching. I do think I got some pretty solid hits on him. Toward the end of this engagement, I had pulled up after another "109" and was hit just under the base of the left windshield with an explosive round. I never saw the aircraft who fired at me, but I suspect that he was below and in front from the angle the shell went in. Among the many fine qualities of the P-38, there were several pieces of quarter-inch armor plate in selected positions around the cockpit, one of which saved my life today. The piece of armor plate was knocked from its mount and fell to the cockpit floor, but it detonated the explosive round in the process.

My flight log shows that I landed in Sardinia after five hours, but continued on home that same day. Strangely enough, we moved from Sardinia to Foggia in order to be closer to the targets in Austria and Southern Germany, but now, on the missions to France, Sardinia was much closer on return.

The five pilots who left today on the "secret mission" actually were en route to England to pick up five "H" model P-38s. These were slightly improved over the G models we have, but more importantly, there were five MORE airplanes.

22ND

This morning we heard of the seaborne invasion by our forces on a spot thirty-five miles south of Rome. Very little news about it was given over the radio. Our pilots were on the alert all day and the planes were loaded with two 500-pound bombs. No mission was called, however. Today was another warm, bright day just as yesterday. Lts. Rodolff and McIntosh returned today from Ajaccio, Corsica, where they had landed after yesterday's mission. Lt. McIntosh claimed one ME-109 destroyed and one ME-109 damaged. Two pilots, Lt. Austin and Lt. Fischer, are still missing.

23RD

A fighter bomber mission was called just after noon. Eleven of our P-38s went up to dive bomb targets of opportunity on the roads in the vicinity of Orte, Italy, where German convoys are attempting to reinforce their forces in the Rome area. When our planes found the primary target overcast, they dropped their bombs on a road near Barisciano, Italy. Several hits and near misses were observed. No enemy aircraft were encountered and only slight flack at one place. All of our planes returned safely. Major Owens paid us a visit this morning. Everyone was quite interested to hear where he had been and what he had done since he left the squadron at Chateaudun. He spent four months in the States, then requested overseas duty again. He was sent to England where he is now operations officer of a wing, assigned to the 9th Air Force. He told what he knew of the whereabouts of some of our old pilots. Major Glenn is in Iceland; Colonel Weltman in San Francisco; Captain Stemen at Dayton, Ohio; Lt. Riley in Los Angeles. Lt. Austin, who has been missing from the mission of the 21st, came in today. He had been down in Sardinia.

24TH

No mission for our planes and pilots today. The men of the squadron carried on their usual duties. The weather was nice.

25TH

Today was as pleasant a day as we have had since we arrived in Italy. A warm sun shone all morning and through most of the afternoon. There was no mission today. Joe E. Brown, the movie star, made a personal appearance in Foggia tonight. A few of our fellows went to see his show and reported it as being very entertaining.

26TH

Again there was no mission scheduled. The weather today was as bad as yesterday was good. A sharp, cold wind blew all morning. Late in the afternoon a very high wind came up, and with it a downpour of rain. About three of the tents in our area blew down during the night.

27TH

It was cold and windy all day today. The sky was clear with only a 3/10 cloud cover at the field. Ten of our P-38s flew a mission as escort for B-17s bombing Montpellier/Frejorgues A/D, France. The formation encountered intense, heavy, accurate flak over the target area, and one B-17 was seen to go down out of control after being hit. Fifteen to twenty ME-109s and FW-190s attacked our P-38s after the bombing and came out on the short end after a 25 minute battle. Lt. Wingrove destroyed an ME-109. We suffered no losses, and all our planes returned safely to the base after refueling in Sardinia.

28TH

Today's mission for eight of our P-38s was to escort B-17s to Aviano A/Ds, Italy. There were no encounters with enemy aircraft and all of our planes returned safely to the base.

COMMENTS 1/28/44: I was not on the mission yesterday when ten or twenty enemy fighters were involved. I was on today's mission and with only eight aircraft up from our squadron, we were fortunate that no enemy aircraft came up. (As a side note, Aviano Airfield is today one of the primary bases for US and NATO forces in that area.)

29TH

The weather continues to be nice. Our planes didn't fly a mission today. This afternoon Joe E. Brown, the movie actor, came out to our field and put on his show. It was very entertaining, especially so because he brought with him an added attraction — the "Andrews Sisters." We had a motion picture at the "Barn" this evening.

30TH

No mission for our planes today. Supply issued the enlisted men any article of clothing they were short — if they had it on hand — and if they had your size. One of those deals in the Army which sends the fellows away talking to themselves, after sweating out about a three hour line. The weather couldn't be better. That warm sun was out all day. M/Sgt. Manor returned to the squadron after his long stay in the hospital.

31ST

Today's mission was to Klagenfurt, Austria with the B-17s. The bombing was good. No enemy planes were encountered and all of our aircraft returned to the base. This was pay day for the men of the squadron. A

27ᵀᴴ FIGHTER SQUADRON   JANUARY 1944

$200.00 war bond was raffled off at a $1.00 a chance. It was won by T/Sgt. Church. Sgt. Share and Cpl. Bell won a $50.00 bond each.

COMMENTS 1/31/44: We could never figure out when the Luftwaffe would or would not respond. This was one of the main aircraft manufacturing plants and, although there was plenty of anti-aircraft fire, their fighters never showed. The weather in the target area was clear and the Alps were visible for a hundred miles or more from our altitude. With all of the snow, they were indeed a spectacular sight.

WAR DEPARTMENT
A.A.F Form No. 5
(Revised)

INDIVIDUAL FLIGHT RECORD

NAME LAWSON, Francis R.
RANK 2nd Lt., A.C.
AERO. RATINGS Pilot
TRANSFERRED FROM
TO _____ DATE _____

MONTH (S) February , 1944
GROUP 1st Fighter Group
ORGANIZATION—Assigned 27th Fighter Squadron
ORG.—Attached for flying
STATION APO # 520

1	2	3	4 PILOT TIME BY AIRPLANE TYPE						5	6	7	8
Date	Duty	Mission Symbol	Attack	Bomb.	Obs.	Pursuit	Cargo	Training	Aircraft Model Symbol	No. of Landings	Other Than Pilot	REMARKS
1	P	A				1:00			F-38F	2		Foggia-Bari
2	P	A				1:00			F-38G	1		Foggia-Local
3	P	A				1:00			"	1		Foggia-Local
3	P	A				1:15			"	1		Foggia-Local
5	P	A				5:00			"	3		Foggia-Bizerte-Elmad-Ajaccio
6	P	A				1:15			"	1		Ajaccio-Naples
8	P	A				0:30			"	1		Naples-Foggia
10	P	A				1:00			"	1		Foggia-Local
13	P	A				1:00			F-38H	1		Foggia-Local
14	P	C				5:15			F-38G	1		Foggia-Verona-Foggia
16	P	A				1:30			"	1		Foggia-Local
18	P	A				0:15			"	1		Foggia-Local
18	P	A				1:15			"	1		Foggia-Local
23	P	C				5:00			F-38H	1		Foggia-Vienna-Foggia

									9	10	11	12
TOTALS									Total pilot time	Total other than pilot	Pilot time nonmilitary airplanes	
This report						26:15			26:15		26:15	
Previous reports this F. Y.						262:15			262:15		260:10	
Totals this fiscal year						288:30			288:30		286:25	
Totals previous years					40:35	26:05	231:00		297:40	14:45		
Totals to date						329:05	26:05	231:00	586:10	14:45		

DUTY SYMBOLS
P—Pilot   B—Bomber   R—Radio operator
CP—Copilot   OB—Observer   PH—Photographer
N—Navigator E—Engineer   O—Other crew
C—Command Pilot G—Gunner   X—Passenger

NOTE.—When the airplane is assigned to an organization other than that to which the individual is assigned or attached for flying show the airplane organization under Remarks, column 8.

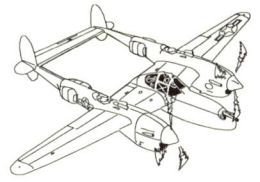

WAR DIARY OF THE 27TH FIGHTER SQUADRON

February 1944

1ST A beautiful day here at the field. There wasn't a cloud in the sky and a warm sun shone the latter part of the morning and all afternoon. There was no mission, as the one scheduled was called of at the last minute. Marseille, France, was to have been the target. Flight Officer Morgan left the squadron today. He was transferred to the 15th Air Force Replacement Center.

2ND Today's mission was called off shortly after briefing. Our planes were to have gone with the B-17s to Budapest, Hungary. Consequently, the pilots had the day off. The weather here at the field was good. Routine duties were carried on by the men of the squadron.

3RD Again today's mission was called off because of the weather at the target. Here at the field it was warm and sunshiny. A number of the men of the squadron are taking advantage of the free lessons in French and Italian that are being given in town at the Red Cross — each language twice a week.

4TH No mission today. Typhoid shots were given to the men of the squadron. The weather started out to be really nice today, but by late afternoon it had turned quite cold and just before midnight a heavy rain started. The first S-2 "bull session" was held in the intelligence tent this evening. It was conducted by Lt. Pelcovits who spoke to an audience of about thirty-five men. A number of favorable comments were heard afterwards which prompted the lieutenant to say that they would be continued three nights a week from now on. Lt. Schnurr will be on his way home in the morning. He is catching a transport at Bari.

5TH Lt. Handleman and Cpls. Stemen and Weitz left yesterday for Chemical Warfare School. The rain which started last night continued off and on throughout the day. A strong, cold wind blew through the camp area, and threatened at any minute to tear every tent loose and carry them away. No combat mission was flown today. Lts. Reynolds and Lawson flew a special search mission to Corsica to look for B-17s reported down there after yesterday's mission. Two new pilots, 2nd Lt. Frank M. Williams and F/O Earl P. Sprengel, joined us today.

COMMENTS 2/5/44: I was only able to get in two combat missions this month, but my flight record shows several "A" missions. The weather was a problem all month long. Today Larry Reynolds and I were sent to look for B-17s scattered all over after yesterday's storm. We climbed up through solid cloud cover coming out on top at about thirty thousand feet. We were navigating by time and distance, with no idea of the upper air winds. When the time arrived, we let down, coming out of the overcast at about five or six thousand feet, with nothing in sight but water. Having missed the entire island of Sardinia we turned due south knowing that we could not miss the continent of Africa. After landing at Bizerte for fuel we continued on to Ajaccio on the northern part of Corsica. No sign of any missing B-17s. Weather on the return trip was no better the next day and we were fortunate in being able to get into Naples. As the diary shows, we did not get home until the 8th.

6TH

The weather that has been forcing cancellation of all the missions in the past few days has descended upon us, it seems. Today, as yesterday, that strong, cold wind was still with us. No mission was flown again today. Yesterday, on a search mission to Sardinia, two 71st pilots ran into fourteen JU-88s carying bombs near the Isle of Capri. The JU-88s, upon seeing the P-38s, jettisoned their bombs and scattered, heading northeast. Unfortunately our men were unable to find them after the JU-88s headed for a convenient cloud cover.

7TH

No mission again today. The weather is still bad—cold and damp. The camp area is a sea of mud. Another iIntelligence "bull session" was held tonight in the S-2 tent with about forty men in attendance. Again it was highly interesting. After giving a summary of the news on the war fronts, Lt. Pelcovits then called on Lt. Wingrove to give the fellows an idea of how a typical mission goes from briefing to interrogation by describing the mission of January 27th. The lieutenant's account of what happened on that day was very thorough. Lt. Pelcovits then closed the session by showing and explaining the bomb strike photos taken on the mission.

8TH

To break our long spell of inactivity of the past week, our planes flew escort for the B-24s bombing Prato R.R. junction and M/Y, Italy. Fourteen of our P-38s went out and thirteen completed the mission. One plane returned early because of mechanical difficulty. No enemy planes were encountered. The bombing was rather poor. After the mission the

FEBRUARY 1944   **WAR DIARY OF THE**

officers had a meeting to make plans for a Club. Lt. Miller was elected President and Lt. Peagram, Treasurer. Lts. Lawson and Reynolds returned this afternoon from Naples where they had set down awaiting better weather.

9 TH The weather throughout the entire day was very poor. A hard rain fell all day and a sharp, cold wind added to the misery. About three o'clock this afternoon our pilots were put on a "stand by." Two five hundred pound bombs were hung on the ships, but the mission never came off.

10 TH The weather improved somewhat and allowed the 71st and 94th Squadrons to fly a mission. They used some of our planes for a dive bombing mission. A 71st pilot flying old "HVX," the oldest plane in the group, was seen to crash when the tail of "X" was blown off by the explosion of the bomb from the plane preceding it into the target. "X" was one of the original P-38s to come overseas with the squadron, having been flown across the ocean by Major (then Lt.) Newbury in June 1942. Captain Butler, Lts. Maron, Ferrin, Flynn, and Maloney returned today from their trip to England. They each flew in a new P-38-H. Eight men: T/Sgts. Smith and Petuch, S/Sgts. Bandfield and Harvey, Sgts. Davidson and Ehrhardt, and Cpls. Dunn and Shores were called up to appear at the Cadet Examining Board in Bari tomorrow morning.

11 TH There was no mission today. The men on the line put in a full day's work on the new "Hs." At a pilot's meeting this morning, Captain Peterson, our Engineering Officer, pointed out the main differences between the new planes and the "Gs" which we have been using for the past year. There have been very few changes made, other than in the engines. The "Hs" will develop more horsepower and should be faster.

12 TH T/Sgt. Petuch and Sgt. Davidson were accepted by the Cadet Board. S/Sgt. Harvey and Cpl. Dunn must return for further examination. The weather remains quite cold. Again there was no mission. The pilots were on "stand by" all day.

13 TH A number of the pilots took the "Hs" up on test flights during the day. The pilots were on "stand by" again today. The weather here at the field and over the target areas have made it impossible to fly a mission. We had a bit of snow this morning. It was very wet stuff and made the camp area muddy. The sun wasn't out long enough to dry things up.

COMMENTS 2/13/44: This was my first flight in the "H." While we were extremely happy to have five more airplanes, I do not recall that they were significantly better than our old "Gs." Maybe it was because of the effort and skill of our maintenance people. The "Hs" had problems as evidenced in the diary entry for the next day.

14 TH Fifteen of our planes were finally able to get off on a mission this morning. Six of them, all but one flying "Hs," returned early because of supercharger trouble. The remaining nine went on with the new B-24 groups who were bombing Verona M/Y, Italy. Our pilots reported that the bombing they saw was not very good. Eight to ten ME-109s and RE-2001s were encountered at the target. They were apparently being engaged by our P-47s who were also along on the mission. As the ME-109s came diving through the formation being pursued by the P-47s, our pilots found it difficult to distinguish between the two. Lt. Reynolds and his flight started out to drive two ME-109s off the tail of a lone B-24, but P-38s from another squadron beat them to it. The last our pilots saw, the B-24 was flying along with all but one engine feathered heading south and west. Tonight at the "bull session," Lt. Pelcovits gave a good summary of the news on all fronts, and then called on Lt. Austin to give the fellows the details of today's mission. About forty-five men attended. Lt. Handelman and Cpls Stemen and Weitz returned from Chemical Warfare School today.

COMMENTS 2/14/44: Obviously with a flight in excess of five hours, I was not one of the "E/R." The difficulty in distinguishing P-47s from an FW-190 was not exaggerated. As I pushed the throttles up and started to turn into what I thought was an FW-190, there was a loud crash; my rear canopy glass was shattered; power on the left engine dropped off to near nothing; I was rolled over on my back, and to make things even worse, smoke was coming up from the bottom part of the cockpit. I was sure that I had taken a hit in the left side, but such was not the case. After all of my favorable comments about how good and reliable the turbo supercharger really was, my left turbo had exploded! Knowing that this might happen, Lockheed had mounted a small piece of armor plate as shown in this drawing.

Engine exhaust gases passed through the turbine (on top) which turned at a very high rate, driving the impeller which, in turn, provided a high volume of air; mixed with fuel allowing the engine to develop full power at very high altitude. Metal used in the turbine and the manufacturing process was quite advanced at that time and was considered a closely guarded secret.

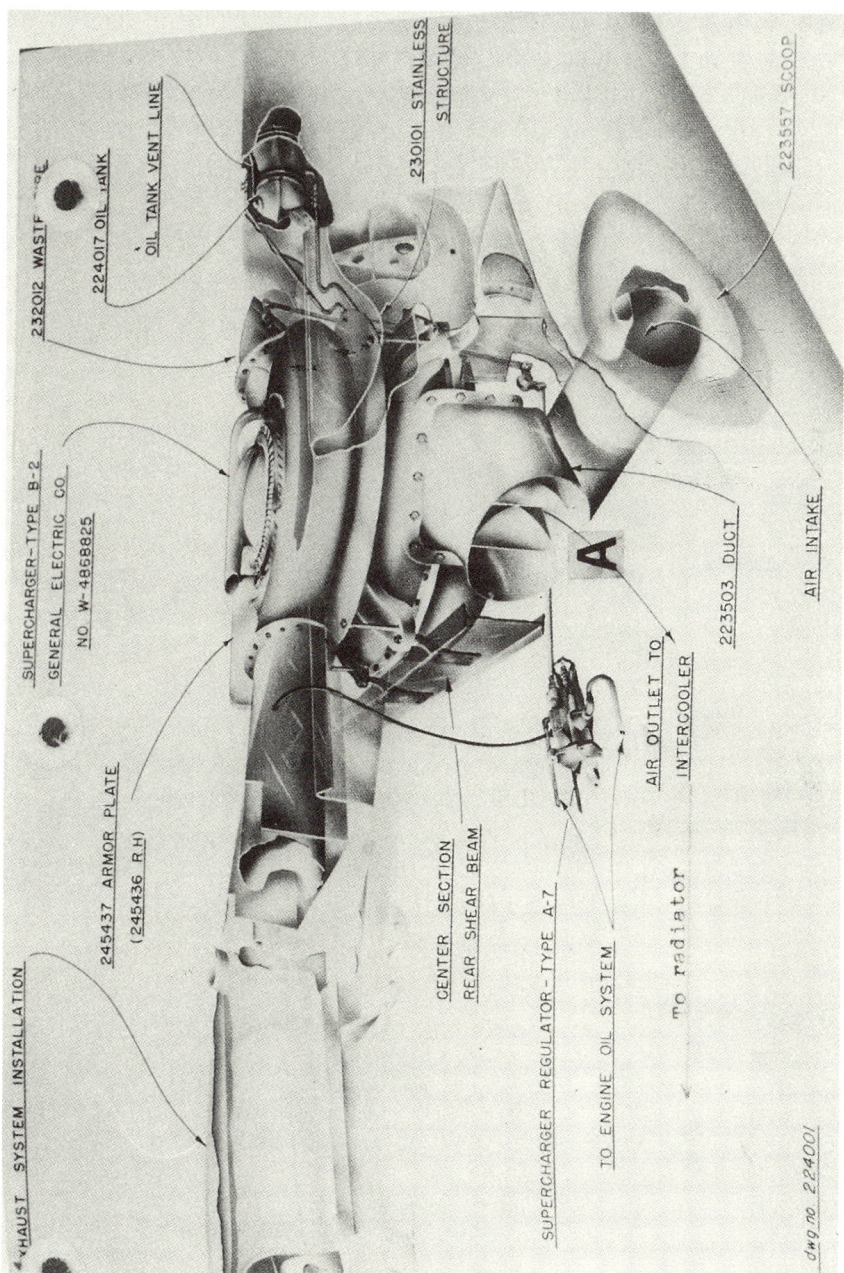

When the turbo exploded, it blew the armor plate off its mount, through the rear canopy and destroyed my radio. The smoke in the cockpit was from one of the red-hot turbine buckets falling down inside my fur-lined flying boot and setting the sheepskin on fire. At that altitude with no supercharger on that side, the left engine power dropped to ambient, while power had been advanced on the right side. It took a few seconds to figure all of this out and, meanwhile, I had lost some ten or fifteen thousand feet.

Separated from the rest of the squadron and with no radio, I had to make it back alone.

15TH

No mission today. S/Sgt. Harvey and Cpl. Dunn were accepted by the Cadet board today. Lt. Handelman is conducting an inspection of all gas equipment. It was very cold all day. A hard driving rain fell throughout most of the morning.

16TH

Our pilots and planes remained on "stand by" all day today, but no mission took place. At the intelligence "bull session" this evening, Lt. Pelcovits, after giving the usual news summary, gave an interesting talk on the composition of the German Army and Air Force. T/Sgt. Dost replaced S/Sgt. Erhard as Mess Sergeant yesterday.

17TH

No mission again today. Usual camp duties were carried on by the men of the squadron. Lt. Laird was awarded the Distinguished Flying Cross on General Order #43, Headquarters 15th Air Force.

18TH The pilots had another day of rest as no mission was flown. The weather was the same as it has been for the past three days—cold and damp in the morning and it doesn't seem to warm up any until late afternoon. Captain Richardson conducted the "bull session" tonight in the intelligence tent. After a resume of the news on the war fronts, the Captain explained the functions of squadron S-2. Sgt. Sam DiLorenzo passed the Cadet Examining Board this morning. He had taken his tests yesterday.

19TH Again there was no mission. This afternoon we had a lot of excitement for a few minutes. Someone in the cockpit of a 94th plane on the ground, pressed the cannon button and fired all sixty shells. There was a great deal of scrambling for cover in our area as the tracers went overhead. Very luckily, no one was injured. There was an Italian circus in Foggia and a number of the men who attended reported it as being good, though falling pretty short of a Ringling Brothers Show, and more like a small carnival show in the States.

20TH Today fourteen of our planes and pilots took off to escort B-17s to Regensburg, Germany. It would have involved a round-trip of over nine hundred miles for our fighters. They were told that the mission was being called off because of weather conditions when they were two hundred miles up the Adriatic coast from our base at Foggia. Our planes re-turned immediately after that, and the pilots had the rest of the day off. This long period of inactivity, lately, has made everyone quite restless. No one can do anything about the weather, however. Again today, it was cold with heavy, low clouds over the field all day.

21ST

Again the scheduled mission was called off. This time shortly after briefing. Our planes were to have escorted the B-17s to bomb Rome's Littorio M/Y. This cancellation, due to the weather at the target, was especially annoying to the pilots, in view of the fact that it is rumored our ground forces in the beachhead area are being hard pressed. They realize, as do all of us, how much help a successful mission of this type could be. One of the interesting things that happened today was M/Sgt. Charlie Wibirt and T/Sgt. Red Everett's foot race. Seems as though these two "old" men were arguing which one was the oldest. "Moose" Wibirt bet "Red" Everett that he could outrun "Red" at five hundred yards. The bet was for $10.00. They were off in a flash and were running neck and neck for twenty-five yards when "Moose" Wibirt fell headlong down the course. "Red" finished the race and picked up the two thousand lire notes at the end of the course. Said Wibirt after the race, "I've been scouting the big Redhead for two years and that's the fastest he's ever moved." M/Sgt. Wibirt has received numerous challenges to another foot race. He claims the sporting blood in the squadron is gone, for everyone challenges the loser and not the winner. Lt. Gerry returned from the hospital today. The subject of the "bull session" this time was: "New developments in German aircraft." About twenty-five men were in attendance.

22ND

Fourteen of our P-38s went out shortly after noon and flew to Volkermarkt, Austria, where they picked up B-24s returning from bombing Regensburg, Germany. Our P-38s escorted the bombers, as well as two stragglers, as far back as Dugi Island on the Yugoslav coast. No enemy planes were encountered. Our planes encountered flak over the Italian coast after leaving the bombers. Luckily, nobody got hit. Italian laborers are putting up two stone buildings in our area which are to be used for an officers' mess, and enlisted mens' club, and for departmental offices. In the past two weeks, there has been nothing but praise for the all-around improvement in the kitchen and in the quantity and quality of the chow. Everyone is agreed that at present we are eating better than at any other time since being overseas. The vote of thanks should go to T/Sgt. Dost, who is doing a very good job as mess sergeant.

23 RD

Our squadron flew today as escort for B-24s withdrawing from bombing Steyr, Austria. Lt. Ferrin led our squadron of twelve planes which picked up the bombers at St. Georgen, Austria, and escorted them back as far as Dugi Island. One B-24 was seen to spin in through the overcast. Another B-24 crew bailed out of their damaged plane. Eight chutes were seen to open. All of our P-38s returned safely. Lts. Wingrove, Alford, and Lawson, and T/Sgt. Scott and Sgt. Cotney are going to leave in the morning for rest camp on the Isle of Capri. These lucky individuals will stay there about a week. At the S-2 "bull session" tonight, Lt. Ferrin, who led the mission today, gave a very descriptive and interesting account of it. Lt. Pelcovits gave the usual summary of the news on the war fronts. The biggest crowd yet, packed the S-2 tent to capacity.

COMMENTS 2/23/44: Another five-hour mission past the snow-covered Alps en route to the Styer/Vienna Austria area. At least we are now able to get a full strength squadron of twelve aircraft up on one mission. Another welcome change was the arrival of electrically heated flight suits. Although criticized by some, I was extremely glad to have one. They were made of material similar to an electric blanket and plugged into a rheostat in the cockpit. On a long, high-altitude mission like today, they were great!

The contrast between our normal existence in the squadron and the conditions in the hotel on the Isle of Capri was almost too good to be true. Clean white sheets on real beds, plenty of hot water for showers, and the best food since leaving the States, all made for a most enjoyable week. Hard to believe I was still glad to get back with the squadron.

24TH

Our squadron flew its 400th combat mission today. Lt. Maron, on his 50th mission, led the squadron of twelve planes which was the lead squadron of the three P-38 groups that escorted the B-17s to bomb Steyr, Austria. The mission was highly successful, as the bombers played havoc with German aircraft factories in that area. All our planes returned safely after the mission. A number of enemy aircraft were seen in the target area, but they were reluctant to mix with our P-38s. The one black spot on the mission was the fact that Lt.Col. McKinzie, the Group Operations Officer, was lost. He was leading the 71st Squadron when about ten minutes after leaving the target he was heard to say over the radio that his plane was afire and he was bailing out. No one saw him after that. The very good motion picture, "Thousands Cheer," was the feature at "The Barn" this evening. Lt. Eickmann left the squadron today. He is going to the HQ & HQ Squadron of the 15th Air Force.

25TH

Today the heavy bombers put on a big show over Regensburg, Germany, and our P-38s acted as escort for B-24s returning from there. At just about the time that the rendezvous with the bombers was made over Radstadt, Germany, the 94th Squadron was heard to give the 71st Squadron's call sign telling them to break, indicating that enemy fighters were coming down on them. Our pilots did not see any enemy planes near them and did not break. When our planes returned to our base, it was learned that an enemy plane was seen to make an attack on the last two planes of our squadron. Lt. Parsons is missing from this action, and Lt. Price, his wing man, was taken to the hospital as soon as he landed. Lt. Price had a very close call. He was struck in the face by flying glass when a shell, fired by an enemy plane, exploded in the cockpit. He was unable to see out of one eye thereafter, but did a beautiful job of flying all the way back and to make a good landing in a rainstorm at our base. The plane was badly damaged. The instrument panel was broken, the cockpit canopy glass shattered, and the armor plate at the back of his head was broken loose by a bullet. There were also two holes through one propeller and the tail assembly had a number of bullet holes in it. Captain Adams, the medical officer, returned from the hospital late tonight and said that Lt. Price was resting easy, but, as yet, they were uncertain of the extent of his eye injury. None of the pilots on the mission could say what had happened to Lt. Parsons, who was last seen just before the action. Lt. Pelcovits told the thirty-five men, who attended the bull session tonight, about the mission today and gave the usual review of the news on the war fronts. The session had to be cut short as a hard rain and windstorm threatened to down the S-2 tent at any moment during the session.

26 TH No mission today so the pilots had the day off. There was no flying; dark threatening clouds hung low over the field all day. It was quite cold and that strong wind continued to blow. A sidearms [pistols] inspection was held today by the ordnance company. An officers' meeting was held this afternoon, and it was announced that the airplane guard would be increased and that an Officer of the Guard would be on every night. On the last two missions the 71st Squadron has lost two planes when they caught fire from an unknown cause, and both under the same circumstances, so the possibility of sabotage cannot be overlooked.

27TH

Another day off for our pilots. There was no flying other than one flight by the "piggyback" in which Lt. Maron took an English sergeant up and engaged a P-47 in a dog fight over the field. Upon landing, the Englishman, when he was able to talk, said he thought that the P-38 was quite a "bloomin' kite!"

28TH

No mission today. About six of the new pilots went up on a training mission this morning. This afternoon the enlisted men beat the officers in a football game to avenge somewhat the defeats in the two previous games. The score was 12-0 today. Sgt. Ladson scored both touchdowns — one on a lateral pass from the ten yard line by Sgt. DiLorenzo — and the other on a thirty-five-yard pass from Sgt. Schneider, which he caught over the goal. The lineups: for the officers: Capt. Goebel, Lts. Reynolds, Rafael, Lienau, Rodolff, Ferrin, Maloney, Cooley, and F/O Sprengel; for the enlisted men: Sgts. Schneider, Wilson, DiLorenzo, Harvey, Meachan, Carlton, Martensen, Ladson, Pasteris, and Pvt. O'Leary. As a trophy, a new football, with the score painted on it, will remain in the enlisted mens' mess until they suffer a defeat at the hands of the officers, at which time it will go to the officers' mess.

29TH

Another day off for the pilots and planes as no combat mission was scheduled. This was payday for both officers and enlisted men. A $100 war bond was won by S/Sgt. Urton and another by Sgt. Martin. Sgt. McConaghy won a $50 bond. We received General Orders #45, Headquarters 15th Air Force, today which awarded Capt. Butler the first Oak Leaf Cluster to the Distinguished Flying Cross, and the Silver Star. First Lt. Charley Brown was awarded the Silver Star on Gen. Orders #47, Hq. 15th A.F. First Lt. Wellner was awarded the

27TH FIGHTER SQUADRON FEBRUARY 1944

DFC on Gen. Orders #11, Hq. 12th A.F. First Lt. Hill was awarded the DFC on Gen. Orders #41, Hq. 15th A.F. First Lts. Maron and Tibble were awarded the DFC on Gen. Orders #56, Hq. 15th A.F. Lt. Wingrove was awarded the DFC on Gen. Orders #50, Hq. 15th A.F.

WAR DEPARTMENT
A.A.F Form No. 5
(Revised)

INDIVIDUAL FLIGHT RECORD

NAME: LAWSON, Francis R.
RANK: 1st Lt., A.C.
AERO. RATINGS: Pilot
TRANSFERRED FROM:
TO: .... DATE ....

MONTH (S): March, 1944
GROUP: 1st Fighter Group
ORGANIZATION—Assigned: 27th Fighter Squadron
ORG.—Attached for flying:
STATION: APO # 520

1	2	3	4 PILOT TIME BY AIRPLANE TYPE						5	6	7	8
Date	Duty	Mission Symbol	Attack	Bomb.	Obs.	Pursuit	Cargo	Training	Aircraft Model Symbol	No. of Land-ings	Other Than Pilot	REMARKS
5	P	A				2:00			F-38H	1		Foggia-Local
7	P	C				6:00			"	2		Foggia-Toulon-Alghero-Foggia.
11	P	C	*1-ME 109 Dest.			7:00			"	2		Foggia-Toulon-Decimomano-Foggia.
15	P	C				2:15			"	1		Foggia-Cassino-Foggia
17	P	A				2:30			"	1		Foggia-Local (ER).
18	P	A				2:30			"	2		Foggia-Local
19	P	C				4:00			"	1		Foggia-Toyer-Foggia
20	P	E				1:00			"	1		Foggia-Local
21	P	E				0:30			F-39J	1		Foggia-Local
25	P	A				1:15			"	1		Algiers-Djedeida
26	P	A				1:45			"	1		Algiers-Djedeida
28	P	A				2:00			"	1		
29	P	A				1:15			"	1		

								9	10	11	12
TOTALS								Total pilot time	Total other than pilot	Pilot time nonmilitary airplanes	
This report				36:00				36:00		36:00	
Previous reports this F. Y.				288:30				288:30		286:25	
Totals this fiscal year				324:30				324:30		322:25	
Totals previous years				40:35	26:05	231:00		297:40	14:45		
Totals to date				365:05	26:05	231:00		622:10	14:45		

DUTY SYMBOLS
P—Pilot   B—Bomber   K—Radio operator
CP—Co pilot   Ob—Observer   PH—Photographer
N—Navigator   E—Engineer   O—Other crew
C—Command Pilot   G—Gunner   X—Passenger

NOTE.—When the airplane is assigned to an organization other than that to which the individual is assigned or attached for flying, show the airplane organization under Remarks, column 8.

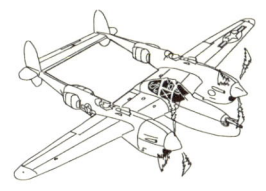

WAR DIARY OF THE 27TH FIGHTER SQUADRON

March 1944

1ST The scheduled mission was called off because of bad weather just before take off time this morning. Our planes were to have escorted formations of B-24s over the Anzio beachhead area, and then remain there acting as an air umbrella for about fifteen minutes while the B-24s and other planes bombed German troop concentrations just beyond our front lines. The pilots were on standby the remainder of the day. The weather over the target evidently failed to clear for the mission was not flown. Early this morning Private O'Leary, one of the airplane guards, caught two young thieves going across the airfield carrying some G.I. equipment they had stolen. They were turned over to the Provost Marshal in Foggia. After a bit of persuasion they talked and implicated a number of others in a ring of thieves, including the leader. A number of enlisted men were promoted today on Special Orders #15, Headquarters, 1st Fighter Group. Cpls. Jesse C. Donne, Robert W. Emerton, Willard Rawlinkiewiez, Charles E. Dungey, and Emil Jariabko were promoted to sergeant. T/5 John C. Shores, Pfc. Donald A. Krook, Pfc. James F. Mathews, Pfc. Richard J. Koos, Pfc. Howard M. LaPlant, Pvts. Bonnie C. Snell, George H. Clark, and Patrick J. O'Leary were promoted to corporal. Lt. Maron was transferred to Headquarters, 1st Fighter Group. He will remain attached to our squadron for rations, quarters, duty and administration.

2ND The same mission that had been scheduled yesterday was flown today. Twelve of our P-38s flew escort patrol for B-24s over the Anzio beachhead area. They remained over the target for forty minutes and did not encounter any enemy aircraft. Our pilots were unable to observe the results of the bombing because of their height. All of our planes returned safely to base. The building in which the officers' and enlisted mens' clubs are to be in, is just about completed. The officers have started to decorate their's already.

3RD Eleven of our P-38s went out this morning to escort bombers to Prato Marshaling Yard, Italy. The bombers did not drop their bombs as they had to turn back just short of the target because of bad weather. The pilots were particularly annoyed at the bombers failure to maintain radio silence to the target. The bomber crews kept up a constant chatter over the interphone channels. Fortunately the enemy failed to capitalize on the bombers lack of caution and no enemy planes were encountered. All of our planes returned safely to our base. A Lieutenant Colonel from the Inspector General's office inspected our camp area, and he also was here to listen to complaints or suggestions anyone might have. A couple of the pilots, when they were asked if they liked the type of flying they were doing, said they would prefer to fly more dive bombing and strafing missions for they felt in that way they could take full advantage of the versatility of the P-38. The Colonel said he would take their suggestions to the proper persons. Lt. Maron was promoted to Captain to rank from 1 March. 1944.

4TH Our P-38s took off just before eight o'clock this morning to escort B-17s of the 5th Wing to the point of the P-38s limited endurance. The B-17s were to continue on from there to bomb Breslau, Germany, which is rumored to be the new seat of the German government. After being out about an hour over Yugoslavia the B-17 leader was heard to say over the radio that they were turning back because of the weather. All our planes returned to base. Nothing of special interest took place in the squadron today. The weather was nice at the field today. It was warm and sunshiny with only a few scattered clouds overhead.

5 TH We had rain here at the field all morning. No mission was scheduled. The officers' club had its opening this evening. The enlisted mens' club is not yet ready, but it should be finished in the next week. S/Sgt. Breton and Cpl. Christensen head the committee doing the arrangements for the enlisted mens' club.

6 TH The scheduled mission was called off just after briefing this morning. It was cold all day here at the field. Dark, heavy clouds hung low overhead. Battle stars for the European, African, Middle East campaign ribbon were issued today. Those men who have been with the squadron since just before November 8, 1942, received three stars. One for the initial landings in North Africa, one for the Tunisian campaign, and one for the Sicilian campaign.

7 TH Today's mission was with the B-17s who were bombing Toulon Harbor, France. Five of our planes returned early, leaving nine of our planes to go all the way with the bombers. About ten minutes before target time between twenty-five to thirty enemy aircraft attacked the formation. They attempted to break through to get at the bombers but were driven off by our P-38s, led by Lt. Wingrove, who probably destroyed an FW-190 in the engagement. Only a few of the bombers were able to find a break in the overcast which would allow them to find their target and bomb it. Lt. Burgoyne and F/O Delaney did not return with the squadron and it is presumed that they are missing. They were last seen in the target area at the time of the engagement with the enemy. S/Sgt. King was reduced to Private.

COMMENTS 3/7/44: With the five early returns, this was a particularly trying mission. All of the flights had to be rearranged en route to the target. No one was able to fly the mission as planned. Once again running short on fuel, I landed in Corsica to refuel before returning. The diary entry sounded as though this was a simple hit and run by the Luftwaffe, but I remember it differently. They attacked repeatedly all the way in to the target and broke off only when the anti-aircraft fire started just before bomb release.

8 TH Lt. Burgoyne and F/O Delaney both returned this afternoon. F/O Delaney flew his plane in, but Lt. Burgoyne came in on a B-17, having left his plane at Ajaccio, where both had landed. The right engine of the plane the Lt. was flying detonated from an unknown cause after he had made two breaks into the enemy planes yesterday. Sgt. Eugene Dunn was transferred to the 61st Station Hospital.

9 TH No mission today. Nothing of special interest took place in the squadron today. The names of the ten men who have been accepted for return to the States under the rotation of troops system was posted on the squadron bulletin board. The fortunate ones are: Sgts. Harrison, Leary, Gardon, Cotney; Cpls. Banchero, Gage; Pvts. Hogan, Felege, O'Meara; Pfc. Walters.

27ᵀᴴ FIGHTER SQUADRON   MARCH 1944

10 TH A hard rain which lasted all day kept our planes from flying a mission. The runway and taxi-strips were under water by this evening. Squadron Supply held a salvage day taking in all worn out clothing and replacing it. The motion picture, "Du Berry was a Lady" was on at the "Barn" this evening. Lts. Ferrin, Austin, Maloney, and McIntosh left for rest camp today. It is on the Isle of Capri.

11 TH Our P-38s made the long trip to Toulon, France, again today. This time they escorted B-24s who did some excellent bombing of the dock areas and of ships in the harbor. Just before reaching the target about eight or ten ME-109s and FW-190s attacked the formation. Our P-38s led by Lt. Flynn engaged the enemy planes and destroyed three of them, Lt. Brown destroying an FW-190 and Lts. Lawson and Miller, an ME-109 apiece. We had no losses, all of our planes returned safely to the base. It must have been a rough day for the Hun. Besides the three our squadron got, one of the other squadrons got another three, while the bombers shot down at least one more, which accounted for just about all the enemy planes seen today. When Lts. Lawson, Flynn, and Brown, who were flight leaders on today's mission, returned to the base, they found they had been promoted to first lieutenant, effective February 26th. The enlisted mens' club had its formal opening this evening. A good time was had by all. There is a radio, a phonograph machine, tables and chairs, and a small bar, make it a nice place to spend these evenings. Perryman's drawings on the wall brighten the room up considerably. Lt. Nichol was also promoted to first lieutenant today to rank from 26 February, 1944. His promotion, as well as Lts. Brown, Lawson, and Flynn's, was made through army headquarters.

COMMENTS 3/11/44: This was a different bunch of Luftwaffe pilots today. First of all, they were flying aircraft that were not camouflaged. The leader (who was in a camouflaged aircraft) stayed up above everything and seemed to be sending in the other "trainees" one or two at a time. I say trainees, because one was inexperienced enough to try a "head on" pass at me—something they never did. He never tried it again because he caught the full impact of four .50 caliber guns and one 20mm cannon full in the face. This was my first confirmed air to air kill and I was very proud of it. I recall that there was no feeling about a "person," but rather that this was a mechanical enemy that was doing his best to stop me.

These missions to southern France were quite long and, with the high power settings in the target area, once again I landed for fuel. This time in Sardinia.

I was very happy to be promoted to first lieutenant. This elevated me once and for all out of the "new man" category.

12TH

No mission scheduled for today. A hard, steady rain lasted all day and made the camp area very muddy. It was rumored that a new table of organization, which would give a lot of the enlisted men an advance in grade, was going to be in effect soon. That would help morale no little. There wasn't a show at the field tonight so a big part of the enlisted men gathered in the club. Sgt. Edmonds returned to the squadron after his very long stay of four months in the hospital.

13TH

The bad weather continues here at the field. We had a light rain this morning, and this afternoon and evening a hard, cold wind made the inside of a warm tent the only comfortable place to be. Our Squadron Commander, Captain Butler, was promoted to the rank of Major, effective March 6th. His promotion came from Headquarters, 15th Air Force. Our planes were idle again today. The weather we have had in the past week has hampered the operations of the whole Air Force, somewhat. Likewise, the operations of our troops on the ground fronts at Cassino and on the Anzio beachhead have been affected by the bad weather. At the S-2 "bull session" this evening Lt. Miller gave a very interesting and informative talk on aircraft instruments. About thirty-five men attended the session. Lt. Pelcovits gave the usual summary of the war news. T/Sgt. Torbett O. Marshall was transferred to the 306th Wing. Sgt. Marshall was one of the old-timers in the squadron and his many friends were sorry to see him leave.

14 TH

Again our planes were idle all day because of the bad weather here at the field. A captain from a P-38 group of the 8th Air Force in England visited the squadron today and talked with a number of the men on the line about what experiences our old pilots had flying the P-38 in close support of ground forces. He told of the conditions in England these days, and when asked when he thought the invasion of the continent would be made, he said you could ask that same question of anyone up to a Four Star General and they wouldn't have any more to say about it than himself—its a tough one to answer, he said. Late this afternoon a notice was posted on the bulletin board saying that it was strongly rumored among the civilians that the Germans were going to bomb Foggia tonight. Taking it for what it was worth, the Wing ordered special precautions to be taken to insure that our blackout was complete.

15 TH

We had an air raid alert about 2:00 A.M. this morning but the "all clear" was sounded ten minutes later. No planes were heard overhead during that period. The 15th Air Force put on a big show over the enemy-held town of Cassino which lasted all day. Formations of B-17s and B-24s were going back and forth from just after daylight until almost dark. Our P-38s flew escort patrol over the target area in two separate missions, one in the morning, and one late this afternoon. Both were uneventful for our squadron in that no enemy planes were encountered on either mission. Our pilots weren't able to observe much of the bombing because of their altitude of 24,000 feet. Tonight's broadcast on the radio said that 2,500 tons of bombs were dropped during the day on an area one mile square in the town. Allied forces had entered the bombed town after the bombers left and they were reported to be making progress. Two good pictures were on at "The Barn" this evening. They were the "Glass Key," and "Shadow of a Doubt."

COMMENTS 3/15/44: As the previous few day's entries show, weather has been a real problem. Particularly discouraging because we knew that the Anzio beach head was very hard pressed. I had mixed feelings about this Cassino mission, what with the monastery being the B-24s target. I wondered why they were not working in direct support of the beach head, but maybe this was close enough to take off some of the pressure. This was really sort of a "milk run" for the fighters because nothing came up toward us, not even any anti-aircraft fire.

16TH No mission was scheduled for today. The weather is starting to get better. We had a bright sun here at the field most of the day. "What's Brewing in the Balkans?" was the subject of tonight's S-2 bull session.

17TH Eleven of our P-38s escorted B-17s to bomb Fischamend Market, Austria. Nine of them made the entire trip, the other two returned early because of mechanical failure. The bombers dropped their bombs through the complete overcast which covered the target area. No enemy planes were encountered and only a little flak on the return, which burst among the bombers. All of our planes returned safely to base.

This was Lt. Meikle's 50th mission. It was a warm, bright day here at the field. The men of the squadron carried on their usual duties. T/Sgt. Wilbur A. Rimer was assigned to the squadron today. He was a radio operator-gunner in the 376th Bomb Group. He had put in fifteen missions in a B-24. Cpl. Collagan returned from a stay in the hospital.

18TH

Nine of our planes took off about 7:30 this morning to fly a sweep over the airdromes in the Udine, Italy, area. To avoid being detected by the enemy radar system, our planes flew the entire distance to the target area at an altitude of about seventy-five feet. The airfield at Treviso was strafed by our P-38s led by Lt. Rafael who shot a JU-52 down in flames over the field. It had just taken off and was about a hundred feet off the ground. Lts. Alford and Gerry destroyed a HE-111 on the ground. Lt. Alford damaged another HE-111, and two more HE-111s were damaged by Lts. Miller and Prout. A train was also strafed by our pilots, the engine of which was later believed to have blown up. Lt. Lindhurst is missing following this action. It is thought that his right wing tip was damaged when he struck a high tension wire. He peeled up to the right instead of to the left with the rest of the squadron. He was not seen after that. The enlisted men of the squadron had a dance in Foggia at the Red Cross Club. The music was furnished by a very good colored orchestra. A good time was had by all, despite the fact that there weren't nearly enough girls. About six American WACs and twenty Italian girls attended. Captain Richardson, Lts. Rodolff and Peterson, and T/Sgts. Kaduk and Smith left for rest camp on the Isle of Capri. Lts. Ferrin, Austin, Maloney, and McIntosh returned this afternoon from rest camp. Cpls. Shores and Stoltzfus and Pvt. O'Meara of the Medics were transferred to Headquarters, 1st Fighter Group, but will remain attached to our squadron for duty temporarily.

19th

Nine of our p-38s were to escort B-17s to Steyr, Austria, but after the rendezvous with the bombers north of Klagenfurt, Austria, they picked up three groups of B-24s flying north toward the target, instead of the B-17s who were homeward bound. Our planes went with the B-24s and escorted them to the vicinity of Steyr, but due to the overcast there, the bombers turned back and bombed Klagenfurt. No enemy fighters were encountered, and all of our P-38s returned safely. Nothing of special interest took place in the squadron today other than the mission.

COMMENTS 3/19/44: This is another one of those days when we wonder why the Luftwaffe did not show up. We were very deep into enemy territory; B-17s and B-24s were strung out for miles and miles, and there we were with a "piddley" little flight of nine P-38s and no one came up to attack. Also, this area of Austria was covered up with aircraft and other related industry factories. The snow-covered Alps stuck up through the overcast like beacons.

20th

No mission was scheduled for today. This was one of the nicest days we have had here at Foggia. Sterling Holloway and his all GI show "Hey Rookie" was put on over in front of "The Barn" this afternoon. It was very good. Not so good though was the unannounced band concert we had in the camp area during the wee hours this morning. Lt. Lienau's talk on "Radar and I.F.F." was the feature of tonight's "bull session" in the S-2 tent. About thirty men were present.

21st

There was no mission again today. Two inspecting officers, one from 5th Wing, and one from 15th Air Force made a very thorough administrative inspection of the squadron departments. They also inspected the tents in the camp area, and the mess hall. The weather continues to be pleasant.

22 ND

Twelve of our planes escorted B-17s to Verona M/Y, Italy. They reported that the bombing was excellent with well-concentrated bursts in the M/Y causing several explosions and fires. Sixteen enemy aircraft were in the target area, but generally avoided combat with our P-38s. Lt. Alford was the only one able to get in a good shot at one. He saw pieces fly off an ME-109 and claimed it as damaged. All of our planes returned safely. Lt. Lawson left this morning for Maison Blanche, Algeria, to be in charge of the detail of men going to assemble new P-38s there. The enlisted men who also left for Algiers are: T/Sgts. Kirchoff and Rentmeister; S/Sgts. Bergander, Clevenger, and Luckenbacker; Sgt. Kzyzanowski.

COMMENTS 3/22/44: Until I read this diary entry I had completely forgotten that I was assigned on temporary duty to Algiers. I certainly was not selected for engineering or command experience! I did learn many valuable lessons while on this project. First and foremost was "just how little I really knew."

These were the first significant replacement aircraft in a very long while and aside from being brand new, they were the much improved "J" model. This was exciting at the time, but only now in retrospect, do I fully realize how badly we needed these airplanes and what they would mean to us.

Many of us thought that the old "G" models were better looking in that the engine nacelle was much more pointed and just seemed "faster" than the "fat" look of the "J" with the intercooler moved from the wing leading edge to a radiator just under each engine. Looks aside, the J had more fuel with 120 gallons in the new leading edge wing tanks. Dive recovery flaps or "speed brakes" under each wing could be extended with no speed restrictions and all but eliminated the compressibility problem, which could occur in a high speed dive.

Advances in turbo supercharger technology provided much better reliability and all but did away with "early returns" due to supercharger malfunction.

New P-38 J models with no camouflage paint. This is a "Stack Down Echelon" normally used before roll in on a ground target.(Smithsonian NASM)

Unlike most fighters of that period, which had wing mounted armament, the .50 caliber machine guns and 20MM cannon on the P-38 were mounted in the nose, directly under the gun sight. This gave it unmatched concentration of fire power. I do not remember how it was done, but the ammo for the cannon was more than doubled in quantity on these new "Js." By this time we did not need to be concerned with camouflage, so these airplanes were bright shining unpainted aluminum which also saved several hundred pounds in weight. All in all—a much improved aircraft!

My flight record indicates that I flew several of these new machines from Algiers up to Djedeida where someone else apparently took them on up to Foggia. I felt very much "at home" in the "J" by the time I got back to the squadron.

23 RD Our planes took off in the rain early this morning to escort B-17s to Steyr, Austria. The mission was called off shortly after the planes had set course apparently because of the weather. It was cold and rainy here at the field all day. The five men who had passed the Cadet Examining Board last month received word this afternoon that they would leave in the morning for Naples and from there go to Casablanca and to return to the States. First Lt. John Phillips from the 306th Fighter Wing, A-2 section, is going to stay with our squadron for about ten days for the purpose of observing our S-2 procedure. Lts. Reynolds, Lienau, and Miller left for rest camp at the Isle of Capri today. At the S-2 "bull session" this evening the timely topic "Air Power and the Coming Invasion" was discussed by Lt. Pelcovits, with Lts. Meikle and Alford adding a couple of interesting views on the possibilities of using the heavy bombers for direct support of ground troops in the event of a crossing of the English Channel by our forces.

24TH Again our planes were sent up to escort B-17s to Austria, but again, they were turned back because of the weather, this time after they had gotten just north of Fiume. The lucky five, T/Sgt. Petuch, S/Sgt. Harvey, Sgts. Davidson and DiLorenzo, and Cpl. Dunn left this morning for Naples on the first lap of their trip back to the States. The stone building that was erected in the camp area to be used for office space has been completed. The orderlies and medics have already moved into it. S-2 started to move in today. It will give these three departments the best setup they have had since being overseas. General Twining, 15th Air Force Commanding General, presented awards to a number of our pilots in a big formal ceremony up in front of Group Headquarters this afternoon. The Silver Star and First Oak Leaf Cluster to the Distinguished Flying Cross were presented to Major Butler. The Distinguished Flying Cross was presented to Capt. Maron, Lts. Wingrove, Reynolds, and McIntosh. The Air Medal was presented to Lts. Alford, Brown, Ferrin, Lawson, Nichol, Meikle, Petersen, Rafael, Austin, Wingrove, Gerry, Maloney, McIntosh, Miller, Prout, Rodolff, and F/O Delaney.

25TH No mission was scheduled for today. Captain Richardson, Lts. Petersen and Rodolff, T/Sgts. Kaduk and Smith returned this evening from the rest camp on the Isle of Capri. Nothing else of special interest took place in the squadron during the day.

26TH Early this morning, eleven of our planes took off to escort B-17s to Steyr, Austria and again the mission was not completed because of the weather. Our P-38s were forced to turn back when they were over northern Yugoslavia and before they had made rendezvous with the bombers. A number of enemy fighters were seen, but our squadron did not report any encounters. A number of enlisted men received promotions today. T/Sgts. Marion E. Clark, Joseph J. Kaduk, Jr., Robert E. Smith, and Woodrow J. Wingo were promoted to Master Sergeant. S/Sgts. Warren K. Perryman and Paul D. Robbins were promoted to Technical Sergeant. Sgts. Paul S. Morris, and Robert E. Wiggins were promoted to Staff Sergeant. Cpls. Douglas J. Egan, Charles A. Embree, Walter B. Jarvis, Henry R. Jonas, and Angelo Giammanco were promoted to Sergeant. All these promotions were made effective today. Over at the enlisted mens' club this evening, M/Sgt. Clark and T/Sgts. Perryman and Robbins paid for everything that was served.

Pasteris, Furr and Clevenger, working on replacement engines. Pierced steel planks known as PSP was used for runway construction and anything else to get up out of the constant mud. Under these conditions, the quality of maintenance was more than amazing. (Photo: Bob Share)

COMMENTS 3/26/44: The promotion of all of these men was very welcome because most had come overseas with the squadron almost two years before and had not been promoted because the squadron was "up to authorized strength." T/Sgt. Perryman was the artist who did all of the "nose art" on the aircraft and paintings in the club.

More than forty years later, Sgt. Perryman designed the 1st Fighter Group Memorial which now stands at the Air Force Museum in Dayton, Ohio. Sadly, Sgt. Perryman did not live to see this handsome granite statue in place at the museum.

27 TH

No mission was scheduled for today. Sgt. Jonas replaced T/Sgt. Dost as Mess Sergeant. Lt. Phillips left us this morning. Major Roth, from the 306th Wing A-2, visited our S-2 office today. At the "bull session" tonight, Lt. Pelcovits' subject was, "A Survey of the Russian Front." About twenty men attended.

28 TH

Effective this morning we are in the 306th Fighter Wing for duty and administration. Once again we transfer out of the 5th Wing with whom we have been since moving to Foggia the latter part of December 1943, when we left the 42nd Wing. Our P-38s escorted B-24s to Mestre M/Y, Italy, this morning. Our twelve planes were intercepted by about twenty-five enemy aircraft consisting of ME-109s, FW-190s, and MA-202s just before teaching the target. In the engagement that followed, Lt. Maloney destroyed an ME-109 and probably destroyed an MA-202. F/O Delaney destroyed an FW-190. Lts. Nichol and Gerry each damaged an ME-109. Lts. Hartwig and Rodolff have not returned from this mission and are considered to be missing. Lt. Rodolff was seen streaming white coolant fluid from the right engine after being attacked by an FW-190, but was still flying level in the area when last observed. Lt. Hartwig was last seen in a luftberry [circling] turn.

29 TH

Twelve of our P-38s, led by Lt. Ferrin, escorted B-24s to Bolzano M/Y, Italy. Eighteen enemy aircraft attempted to attack the bombers before the target had been reached. They were taken by surprise by our P-38s and as they passed in front of our formation, Lt. Ferrin fired at all of them. He was unable to observe the results. Lt. Prout probably destroyed an ME-109. In this engagement, Lt. Brown was hit and his right engine caught fire. He was last seen in a spiral from 22,000 feet, south of Vicenza, Italy.

Lieutenants Rafael, Lawson, and Brown just a few weeks before Lt. Brown was shot down on March 29th.

MARCH 1944   **WAR DIARY OF THE**

COMMENTS 3/29/44: The following statement was filed concerning this incident:

CONFIDENTIAL

27TH FIGHTER SQUADRON
1ST FIGHTER GROUP
Foggia #3

29 March, 1944.

S T A T E M E N T

    I was flying on Lieutenant Brown's right wing and we were in a medium right bank. Lt. Brown was firing at a ME-109, which was in firing range, when another ME-109 attacked both Lt. Brown and myself from about 4 o'clock, slightly above and closing in to a very close range. I saw the right engine of Lt. Brown's plane burst into flame and from the loss of power of that engine his right wing dropped. The whole plane disappeared from my view as he was beneath my plane.

Robert E. Austin

Incl - 1   ROBERT E. AUSTIN,
                          2nd Lt., Air Corps,
                          27th Fighter Squadron

CONFIDENTIAL

30TH

Eleven of our planes escorted B-17s to Sofia, Bulgaria. Fifteen or twenty enemy planes were observed in the target area but for one ME-109 which attacked Lt. Burgoyne when he had an engine cut out, there was little activity. The lieutenant turned into the enemy plane which immediately broke off combat. All of our planes returned safely. Work has been started on a squadron shower to be set up behind our administration building.

31ST

No mission was scheduled for today. The weather was warm and clear here at Foggia. A lot of P-38s, B-17s, and B-24s were overhead all day on practice flights. This was also payday for the officers and enlisted men. This evening the Articles of War were read to the enlisted men and, after that, all the men went through the gas chamber to test gas masks. Eleven new pilots joined the squadron today. They are: 1st Lt. Jim L. Kuykendall, 2nd Lts. Duane B. Enyeart, Stanley W. Lau, John M. King, Richard M. Huber, John J. K. C. Kim, Edward D. Ulrich, William H. Caughlin, George H. Plummer, Phil E. Tovrea, Jr., and John J. Janson.

WAR DEPARTMENT
A.A.F Form No. 5
(Revised)

INDIVIDUAL FLIGHT RECORD

NAME LAWSON, Francis R.
RANK 1st Lt., A.C.
AERO. RATINGS Pilot
TRANSFERRED FROM _____
TO _____ DATE _____

MONTH (S) April , 1944
GROUP 1st Fighter Group
ORGANIZATION—Assigned 27th Fighter Squadron
ORG.—Attached for flying _____
STATION APO # 520

1	2	3	4 PILOT TIME BY AIRPLANE TYPE							5	6	7	8
Date	Duty	Mission Symbol	Attack	Bomb.	Obs.	Pursuit	Cargo	Training		Aircraft Model Symbol	No. of Landings	Other Than Pilot	REMARKS
2	P	A				3;00				F-38J	2		Casablanca-Oran-Algiers.
3	P	A				3:45				"	2		Algiers-Djedeida-Fog.
4	P	C				4:00				F-38H	1		Foggia-Bucharest-Fog.
5	P	C				4:15				"	1		Foggia-Bucharest-Fog.
6	P	C				4:15				F-38J	1		Foggia-Zagreb-Foggia
6	P	A				0:15				"	1		Foggia-Local
7	P	A				0:30				"	1		Foggia-Local
~~Strikethrough~~						2:00				~~x~~	2		~~strikethrough~~
8	P	A				1:15				F-38F	2		Foggia-Bari-Foggia
9	P	A				1:00				F-38G	1		Foggia-Local
9	P	A				1:15				F-38F	1		Foggia-Local
10	P	A				1:00				F-38G	1		Foggia-Local
11	P	A				3:00				F-38J	2		Foggia-Local
12	P	C				4:45				F-38G	1		Foggia-Weiner Neustad-Foggia.
13	P	A				0:45				F-38J	1		Foggia-Local
14	P	T				1:00				F-38F	1		Foggia-Local.
15	P	E				0:30				F-38J	1		Foggia-Local.
16	P	A				0:15				F-38F	1		Foggia-Local.
16	P	A				2:15				"	1		Foggia-Ajaccio.
16	P	A				2:00				"	1		Ajaccio-Foggia.
16	P	A				0:30				"	1		Foggia-Local.
17	P	A				2:00				"	1		Foggia-Local.
18	P	C				4:30				F-38J	1		Foggia-Udine-Foggia.
19	P	A				1:00				"	1		Foggia-Local.
20	P	C				4:00				F-38G	1		Foggia-Padua-Foggia.
21	P	T				1:00				F-38G	1		Foggia-Local.
23	P	C	* 1-ME 109 Dest			5:00				F-38J	1		Fog-Weiner Neustadt-F

	Attack	Bomb.	Obs.	Pursuit	Cargo	Training	Total pilot time	Total other than pilot	Pilot time on military airplanes
TOTALS									
This report				57:00			57:00		57:00
Previous reports this F. Y.				324:30			324:30		322:25
Totals this fiscal year				381:30			381:30		379:25
Totals previous years			40:35	26:05	231:00		332:40 / 307:40	14:45	55:30
Totals to date	219.25			422:05	26:05	231:00	714:10 / 679:10	14:45	434:55

* DUTY SYMBOLS
P—Pilot   N—Bomber   R—Radio operator
CP—Copilot OH—Observer PH—Photographer
N—Navigator E—Engineer O—Other crew
C—Command Pilot G—Gunner X—Passenger

NOTE.—When the airplane is assigned to an organization other than that to which the individual is assigned or attached for flying, show the airplane organization under Remarks, column 8.

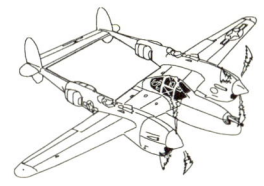 # WAR DIARY OF THE 27ᵀᴴ FIGHTER SQUADRON

April 1944

1ˢᵀ The scheduled mission to Vicenza, Italy, was called off just after briefing, because of the wind around this area, which was so strong that the bombers could not take off. The men of the squadron carried on their usual duties. The intelligence officer, Capt. Richardson, and Lt. Pelcovits, had a session with the new pilots which lasted all afternoon. Each man got a Coca Cola in the rations today—for most of us it was the first in over a year and a half. Lt. Gerry received word today that he was the father of a baby girl.

2ᴺᴰ Fourteen of our P-38s went out this morning to provide withdrawal escort for B-24s bombing Steyr, Austria. About thirty miles short of the target, approximately forty-five enemy aircraft in two groups of twenty and twenty-five attempted to attack the bombers, but were driven off by the P-38 escort. Our squadron destroyed four, probably destroyed another, and damaged one. Our pilots claiming victories were: Lt. Alford, an ME-109 destroyed; Lt. Prout, an ME-109 destroyed; Lt. Nichol, an ME-109 destroyed; Lt. Gerry, an ME-109 destroyed; Lt. Rafael, an ME-109 probably destroyed; and Lt. Cooley damaged an ME-109. All of our planes returned safely. This was a big day for the 15th Air Force as a number of records were broken on this mission principally in the number of bombers over the target and in the number of enemy planes downed; one hundred fifty-seven were claimed "destroyed."

3RD Lt. Lawson returned from Maison Blanche, Algeria, this morning. Two new pilots, 2nd Lts. James M. Joye and James M. Lilly were assigned to the squadron today. S/Sgts. Bohn and Larsen, and Sgt. Gaynor returned from Sidi Ahmed, Tunisia this afternoon. On today's mission our P-38s escorted B-17s to Budapest, Hungary. Ten minutes before reaching the target, the formation was attacked by about 30 enemy planes including ME-109s, FW-190s, ME 210s, and ME 410s. In the engagement Lt. Miller destroyed an FW-190. That was the only claim by our squadron. All our planes returned safely. The bombing of the Hungarian capital appeared to have done considerable damage as smoke and dust rose to five thousand feet. As if a tremendous explosion had taken place.

COMMENTS 4/3/44: The stay back in Africa had been interesting in that I learned a lot about how aircraft are put together and I had the opportunity to fly into several places that I had missed the first time passing through.

I was very happy to be back with the squadron, and quickly realized that I had missed out on some very "productive" missions. We now had sufficient aircraft to put up full strength missions and even a couple of "spares."

4TH Early this morning our P-38s went out to furnish penetration escort for B-17s and B-24s en route to bomb Bucharest, Rumania. The escort was provided without incident, our P-38s going to the point of their limited endurance which was just across the Danube River in Rumania. It was reported later this evening that the bombers had done great damage to the M/Y and adjoining areas of Bucharest. A big air

27ᵀᴴ FIGHTER SQUADRON   APRIL 1944

battle had also taken place. Lts. Wingrove and Meikle were relieved of assignment to the squadron and transferred to the 15th Air Force Replacement Center to await transportation back to the United States.

5ᵀᴴ

This afternoon our P-38s provided withdrawal escort for B-17s and B-24s returning from bombing Ploesti, Rumania. After making rendezvous with one group of returning B-24s, our P-38s were attacked by about ten ME-109s. The enemy planes taking advantage of the scattered cloud cover used hit and run tactics. Lt. McIntosh's plane was damaged in the encounter. He was forced to make a belly landing at the base because his hydraulic system was shot out. All of our other planes returned safely. No claims were made.

6ᵀᴴ

Lt. Ferrin led the squadron on his 50th mission today. Our P-38s escorted the 461st Bomb Group of B-24s on their first mission to Zagreb, Yugoslavia. No encounters took place though one B-24 was seen to go down in the water off the Yugoslav coast evidently having been damaged by enemy ground fire. Lt. Ferrin, and his wing man Lt. Ulrich, circled the ditched plane and its crew, giving "Mayday" calls. We heard later this evening that the men from the bomber were picked up and are safe. Cpl. Calvin H. Webb was reduced to the grade of Private.

COMMENTS 4/6/44: Having been gone for several weeks, I was given the opportunity to sort of catch up—with three missions in three days. I don't remember much about this except it was rare to get two missions in succession to the same area (Romania).

The mission on the 6th was my first flown in a "J" and the improvements were dramatic. We quickly found out that it would be necessary to keep the same model aircraft in each flight.

With Lt. Wingrove and Meikle returning to the States, I realized that my bunch were some of the "oldest" members still assigned to the squadron. Our return home could not be far behind.

7 TH Today's mission to Treviso, Italy, as escort for B-17s bombing the M/Ys there, was uneventful for ten of our P-38s. No enemy planes were encountered and all of our planes returned safely to base. The pilots reported that smoke billowed up to 8,000 ft. following the bombing. Capt. Goebel, Lts. Campion and Pegram, M/Sgt. Jasonowski, and T/Sgt. Snow left for rest camp at Capri.

8 TH The bad weather today canceled the scheduled mission. Major Butler returned from rest camp this afternoon. Lt. Reynolds was put on Detached Service with Headquarters, 15th Air Force. We had our first look at the new P-51 B when a number of them were over our field this afternoon.

9 TH Easter Sunday—the second the squadron has spent overseas— was a warm bright day. A number of the men were able to go into Foggia to church service this morning. No mission was flown today. Another new pilot, Robert P. Rasmussen was assigned to the squadron today. T/Sgt. Rentmeister, and S/Sgts. Clevenger and Davis returned from Algiers this afternoon where they have been helping to assemble some of the new P-38-Js we have been getting.

COMMENTS 4/9/44: The new pilot, Lt. Rasmussen, who was assigned today moved into our tent and is remembered because of his unusual background. He had served as a crew chief with the Flying Tigers in China and upon returning to the States went into the Aviation Cadet program. Having lived through the war in China, it was even more regrettable that he was killed in action a short while later in May. Faces are changing every day, as more and more new pilots are assigned.

10 TH Only a training flight by the new pilots was flown today. At the intelligence "bull session" this evening, Lt. Pelcovits, after giving a summary of the news on the war fronts, inaugurated a new series of talks entitled, "Know your Enemy." The particular subject tonight was, "What makes a Nazi." In covering this story, Lt. Pelcovits told the story step by step of the National Socialist Party's rise to power in Germany through to the time the Germans marched into Poland. Three more new pilots joined us today. They are 2nd Lts. Harry E. Noone, Warren E. Perry, Galen J. Rhoades.

11 TH No combat mission was scheduled for today. All three squadrons of the group flew a training mission together this afternoon. They practiced formation flying at altitude. The new P-51s which are stationed at a nearby field attacked the formation and engaged our P-38s in simulated combat. The medics gave out atabrine tablets at supper tonight thereby getting an early start in the fight against malaria which is supposed to be very prevalent in this part of the country during the warm months. Lt. Reynolds left to return to the United States.

12 TH Major Butler left us this morning. He is going to return to the United States. Lt. Rafael was appointed Squadron Commander. Lt. Maloney becomes Operations Officer. Our planes escorted B-24s to Bad Voslau, Austria. The results of the bombing were not observed as our planes did not go directly over the target. About twelve enemy fighters were encountered during the mission but they were not eager to engage our P-38s. No claims were made. Lt. Kim did not return from this mission, though we heard later this evening he was down safely at Vis Island, Yugoslavia. T/Sgt. Kirchoff, S/Sgt. Bergander, and Sgts. Boyer and Kzyzanowski returned from Algiers this afternoon.

COMMENTS 4/12/44: The mission today was almost five hours; quite long for one of the older "G" models that I was flying. Bad Voslau, and Weiner Neustadt are near Vienna, Austria, which has one of the primary manufacturing plants for the ME-109 fighter. We were always happy to see strikes in that area.

The departing Major Butler was the same Lt. Butler who had briefed us the first day we arrived in the squadron back in August. Of course both Tom Rafael and Tom Maloney were well known and liked, so we were all very pleased with their promotions.

13 TH

This morning our planes escorted B-17s to Gyor, Hungary. A few enemy planes were encountered when they attempted to attack the bombers, but our P-38s drove them off. An enemy four-engine transport plane was seen escorted by about seven RE-2001s. Our planes dived down from their altitude of 21,000 feet to 7,000 feet. To attack but the transport had disappeared by then. One of the RE-2001s was destroyed and another two probably destroyed. Two more were damaged. Lt. Miller was credited with the destroyed, Lts. Lineau and Prout with the probables, and Lts. Gerry and Austin with the damaged. Our pilots thought the bombing was excellent. We heard late this evening that Lt. Kim had been badly burned when his plane crashed in taking off from Vis Island. After the mission yesterday, Lt. Kim was forced to land on the Partisan-held Island because he was short of fuel. After refueling, Lt. Kim attempted to take off on the very short runway there. When he was about two hundred feet above the ground, one engine sputtered and quit and the plane crashed, catching fire immediately. Lt. Kim was pulled from the wreckage though not before he had sustained serious burns about the face and hands. Also very unfortunate, was the fact that the crash killed seven partisan soldiers and wounded another twenty, who were part of a column marching across the field at the time.

14TH

No mission was flown today. Word was received late this morning that Lt. Kim had died from the injuries received in his crash the day before yesterday. Lts. Campion, Handelman, and Pegram were promoted to 1st Lts. Lt. Campion and Handelman's promotions are effective March 31st, and Lt. Pegram's is effective April 2nd. Captain Adams, and Lts. Burgoyne and Cooley left for rest camp on the Isle of Capri this morning.

COMMENTS 4/14/44: The death of Lt. Kim was particularly hard to take. I always felt this was a very unnecessary accident. Vis was a small field, marginal even under the best of circumstances. Lt. Kim was not an experienced pilot and the servicing of his aircraft at Vis may not have been the best. I wish that we could have flown another pilot up in the "piggyback" and brought Kim out that way. Hindsight is always perfect.

15TH

Our P-38s acted as withdrawal escort for B-24s returning from bombing Bucharest, Rumania. Seventeen enemy planes were seen at different times and places during the mission. A number of these were JU-88s which evaded our planes by taking cover in the clouds. Lt. Maloney fired at an ME-109 but was unable to observe the results because of the clouds. He claims the enemy plane as damaged. All our planes returned safely. Capt. Goebel, Lts. Campion, and Pegram, M/Sgt. Jasinowski and T/Sgt. Snow returned from the Isle of Capri this evening.

16TH

The mission for our planes was one of the longest flown from this base. Twenty of our P-38s took off very early this morning to escort B-24s to Brasov, Rumania. During the long trip only three enemy planes were seen and one of them, an SM-79 transport was destroyed by Lt. Gerry. There were no other encounters, and all of our planes returned safely to base. The first group of enlisted men on the rotation list left this afternoon to start their trip back to the United States. Those leaving were: Sgts. Gardon, Harrison, and Leary; Cpls. Banchero and Gage; Pfc. Walters and Pvts. Felege and O'Meara.

17TH

Our planes escorted B-17s to Belgrade, Yugoslavia. The results of the bombing were not observed. Not a single enemy plane was seen during the mission. All of our planes returned safely to base. The enlisted men had a dance this evening at the Red Cross Club in Foggia. The music was furnished by a colored Special Service band. Just as was the case at the last dance, there weren't enough girls to go around. During the middle of the evening two loud explosions, probably caused by a bomber crash at Foggia Main, broke a number of windows in the Red Cross building and frightened away what few partners there were. Another dance has been scheduled for the 23rd of April. Lt. Miller was promoted to 1st Lt. effective March 26th.

COMMENTS 4/17/44: The diary entry "frightened away what few partners there were" brings to mind the comment by one of the crew chiefs who said: "When the windows were blown out, romance flew out the window."

18TH

On today's mission our P-38s led by Lt. Rafael took off this afternoon to strafe the dispersal area on the Udine/Compoformido A/D, Italy. The weather en route to the target and on the return route was extremely bad. Lt. Rafael did an exceptionally good job of finding the target and leading the squadron back to base without a loss. In strafing the airfield our planes destroyed seven aircraft and damaged eight others. A barge in the Gulf of Panzano was also strafed with unobserved results. The weather here at the field was very good. Nothing of special interest took place in the squadron today.

COMMENTS 4/18/44: If it is possible that the level of concentration influences the degree to which something is imprinted in ones memory, then I understand why this mission is so clearly recalled. Weather was indeed "extremely bad." All the way up the Adriatic coast, clouds were from 300 to 1000 feet with a steady rain reducing visibility. I was leading Blue flight, which is the third flight in the squadron. Two other squadrons, the 94th and 71st, were ahead of us. About half way up the coast, everyone turned around, except us! Meeting a stream of aircraft head on in that kind of weather is not something that one soon forgets. Anyway, we continued on and, as luck would have it, came out lined up perfectly for a strafing run on a major German airfield. They were caught completely unaware. Mechanics were jumping off work stands, and people were running in all directions to get to their anti-aircraft weapons.

I was able to get in a good long burst on an HE-111, twin engine bomber, which was quickly engulfed in flames. As we pulled up at the far end of the airfield, I looked back to check on my wing man, F/O Delaney, and saw him streaming white coolant vapor from his left engine. I called out to him that it appeared that he had been hit and to "feather" his left engine. He promptly did so, and turned right, away from the rest of the squadron. I turned back to pick him up and we were thus separated from the rest of the squadron and missed out on the barge strafing.

The trip home was a little bit slower with Delaney on only one engine. At one point he released his canopy and seemed to be ready to bail out, but fortunately changed his mind.

After landing back at Foggia, we removed the cowling on the left engine and there lay a spent .50 Caliber bullet which had cut the coolant line. The Germans did not use .50 Cal. Guns so the first suspects were my number three and number four man in Blue flight. They of course swore innocence, but the gun camera film from number four clearly showed Delaney's airplane dead center in a stream of tracers hitting the ground just beneath him. One of number four's ricochets had done the dirty deed!

Gun cameras are nice to have. Mine showed an ME-110 parked just past the HE-111 that I burned and the fire got to it also. I had not seen it and did not enter a claim until I saw the film. Contrary to the last sentence in the diary entry, quite a lot took place of special interest.

19 TH

Our planes and pilots had a day off today, no combat mission was flown. T/Sgt. Gawenda and Sgt. E. Dunn returned to the squadron after long stay in the hospital.

20 TH

Sixteen of our P-38s escorted B-17s of the 5th Wing to railway targets at Vicenza, Padua, and Castelfranco, in north Italy. The mission was uneventful. This was one of the warmest days we have had here at Foggia. The men of the squadron carried on their usual duties.

21 ST

Twenty of our P-38s went out this morning to act as withdrawal escort for B-17s returning from bombing Bucharest and Ploesti, Rumania. Shortly after crossing the Yugoslavian coast, the bombers called our Squadron Leader, Lt. Flynn, and said they were returning to base because of the weather. Our planes turned back and landed at our base. Lt. Williams and F/O Springel left for rest camp on the Isle of Capri this morning. Shortly before noon everyone was alerted and told to have guns, helmets, and gas masks readily available for the next two days. No one seems to know just what the reason is, as our group is the only one in the area alerted.

22ND

No combat mission was flown today. A number of the new pilots went up on a local training flight. Captain Adams, Lts. Burgoyne, and Cooley returned from rest camp. A big bunch of the enlisted men attended the weekly "Bingo" game at the special service center, the "Barn." We had a light rain this evening which lasted until about midnight.

23RD

Our planes, on a mission to Bad Voslau, Austria as escort for the B-24s, had a field day at the expense of the Luftwaffe. When the final count was taken, the totals were: six destroyed, two probably destroyed and six damaged. All this without loss to ourselves. Those credited with aircraft destroyed are: Lt. Maloney an ME-110 and an FW-190, Lt. Lawson an ME-109, Lt. Joye an FW-190, Lt. Lilly an ME-110, and Lt. Gerry an FW-190. The pilots who claimed probables were: Lt. Delaney and Lt. Lienau. Damaged aircraft were claimed by Lt. Lau, Lt. Tovrea, Lt. Lilly, Lt. McIntosh, and two by Lt. Maloney. Another dance for the enlisted men was held at the Red Cross Club in Foggia. This time the affair was a real success and a good time was had by all. About five American WACs and fifty Italian girls were present.

COMMENTS 4/23/44: Sufficient numbers and improved performance of the "J" models made this an extremely good day for us. No report is indicated as to how many Luftwaffe fighters were up, but the mixture of type (ME-109, ME-110, and FW-190) had to mean that they threw everything that they had into the fight.

A flight of three ME-109s started a pass on the bombers that we were escorting and I turned into them. From a long way out, I drew a large lead on the flight leader and opened fire, primarily in the hope of firing in front to break him off. Much to my surprise, I saw several explosions just behind his cockpit and he went down trailing flame. Probably my 20MM canon fire did the job. His two wingmen promptly broke away before I could get another shot. As he had been on the April 18th mission, F/O Delaney was on my wing and he got a "probable." The diary mistakenly lists him as "Lieutenant," but he was not promoted until later.

With the extended range of the P-38-J, we could sustain a prolonged flight at high power settings, complete a five-hour mission, and make it all the way home without landing short for fuel. Things were really looking up!

Today's mission was a good way to "complete" this chapter and enabled me to leave with a sense of satisfaction!

"FINITO"

WAR DIARY OF THE 27ᵀᴴ FIGHTER SQUADRON

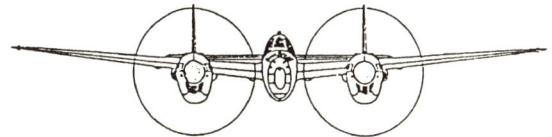

Epilogue

The mission on April 23rd marked the end of my flying with the 27th Fighter Squadron. A few days later, I left to begin the long "boat ride" back to the United States. Of course, the squadron went on to serve for the rest of the war, and even until this day.

Most of the people returned to civilian life at the end of WWII, some to very successful careers. Some of us remained in the Air Force and served in the Korean war as well as in South East Asia (Viet Nam War).

Even though the P-38 was probably the finest fighter to be produced during the war, more than one third of all of the assigned pilots, during the period June 1942 through June 1945, were either killed in action or prisoners of war. No one can truthfully claim that this was not one of the major areas of battle.

Many good and lasting friendships were established during this period. Although the numbers grow smaller each year, the 27th Fighter Squadron Historical Association still enjoys a membership of more than one hundred, who gather every other year for a reunion. After more than fifty years, they still come from all over the United States to attend.

Wars are cruel and wasteful of human life and property. They bring out the darkest side of human nature. However, good people are inspired to their best. This was the worst of times; it was also the best of times. Having lived during that period, I would not have missed it for the world!

In the following quotation, Shakespeare's King Henry says it best:

"BE IN THEIR FLOWING CUPS FRESHLY REMEMBERE'D. THIS STORY SHALL THE GOOD MAN TEACH HIS SON; AND CRISPIN CRISPIAN SHALL NE'ER GO BY, FROM THIS DAY TO THE ENDING OF THE WORLD, BUT WE IN IT SHALL BE REMEMBERED: WE FEW, WE HAPPY FEW, WE BAND OF BROTHERS. FOR HE TO-DAY THAT SHEDS HIS BLOOD WITH ME SHALL BE MY BROTHER; BE HE NE'ER SO VILE, THIS DAY SHALL GENTLE HIS CONDITION: AND GENTLEMEN IN ENGLAND NOW A-BED SHALL THINK THEMSELVES ACCURSED THEY WERE NOT HERE, AND HOLD THEIR MANHOODS CHEAP WHILES ANY SPEAKS THAT FOUGHT WITH US UPON SAINT CRISPIN'S DAY."

ABOUT THE AUTHOR

Francis Robert Lawson, Colonel US Air Force (Ret.) was born in Montgomery, Alabama, on 11 October, 1923. He grew up on a farm in that area and, at age 18, enlisted in the Army Air Corps Aviation Cadet program. Following operational training on Curtis P-40 fighters, he was posted to North Africa in the summer of 1943. How he wound up in the 27th Fighter Squadron and his subsequent war time experiences are the subject of this "Diary."

After World War II, he held various assignments in Aircraft Maintenance and Flight Test, including more than a year in Korea at the beginning of that war. Peacetime duties over the next few years took him to Europe and many U.S. Bases as Operations Officer and Commander of several fighter squadrons. After graduating from The Industrial College of The Armed Forces at Ft. McNair, D.C., he was assigned as a fighter pilot in an F-105 squadron in southeast Asia.

Upon retiring from the Air Force in 1970, he returned to his hometown where he worked as Chief Pilot of a major corporation for another fifteen years. Now fully retired, he and his wife, Sarah, reside in Montgomery, Alabama.